TOGETHER

How We Belong

Troll Target Series

TROLL TARGET SERIES

Lewis Gardner   *Senior Editor*
Miriam Rinn   *Editor*
Virginia Pass   *Teaching Guides*
Cris Peterson   *Bibliographies*
Shi Chen   *Cover Illustration*

PROJECT CONSULTANT

David Dillon   *Professor of Language Arts,*
                   McGill University, Montreal

ACKNOWLEDGEMENTS

"A Failure to Communicate" from *Dave Barry Is Not Making This Up* by Dave Barry. Copyright © 1994 by Dave Barry. Reprinted by permission of Crown Publishers, Inc.

"A Uniform Image" printed with the permission of the author. Copyright © 1997 by Miriam Rinn.

(Acknowledgements continued on page 159)

Contents

A Failure to Communicate

by Dave Barry

Dave Barry is a noted humorist whose columns appear in newspapers all over the United States. He often writes in exaggerated terms about the zaniness of everyday life and the ludicrous things people do without thinking. This wry look at teenage life is definitely from the perspective of a perplexed parent.

Now that my son has turned 13, I'm thinking about writing a self-help book for parents of teenagers. It would be a sensitive, insightful book that would explain the complex, emotionally charged relationship between the parent and the adolescent child. The title would be: *I'm a Jerk; You're a Jerk.*

The underlying philosophy of this book would be that, contrary to what you hear from the "experts," it's a bad idea for parents and teenagers to attempt to communicate with each other, because there's always the risk that one of you will actually find out what the other one is thinking.

For example, my son thinks it's a fine idea to stay up until 3 A.M. on school nights reading what are called "suspense novels," defined as "novels wherein the most positive thing that can happen to a character is that the Evil Ones will kill him *before* they eat his brain."

My son sees *no connection* between the fact that he stays up reading these books and the fact that he doesn't feel like going to school the next day.

"Rob," I tell him as he is eating his breakfast in extreme slow motion with his eyes completely closed, so that he sometimes accidentally puts food into his ear, "I want you to go to sleep earlier."

"DAD," he says, using the tone of voice you might use when attempting to explain an abstract intellectual concept to an oyster, "you DON'T UNDERSTAND. I am NOT tired. I am . . . *sploosh*" (sound of my son passing out facedown in his Cracklin' Oat Bran).

Of course psychologists would tell us that falling asleep in cereal is normal for young teenagers, who need to become independent of their parents and make their own life decisions, which is fine, except that if my son made his own life decisions, his ideal daily schedule would be:

Midnight to 3 A.M.—Read suspense novels.

3 A.M. to 3 P.M.—Sleep.

3:15 P.M.—Order hearty breakfast from Domino's Pizza and put on loud hideous music recorded live in hell.

4 P.M. to midnight—Blow stuff up.

Unfortunately, this schedule would leave little room for, say, school, so we have to supply parental guidance ("If you don't open this door RIGHT NOW I will BREAK IT DOWN and *CHARGE IT TO YOUR ALLOWANCE*"), the result being that our relationship with our son currently involves a certain amount of conflict, in the same sense that the Pacific Ocean involves a certain amount of water.

At least he doesn't wear giant pants. I keep seeing young teenage males wearing *enormous* pants; pants that two or three teenagers could occupy simultaneously and still have room in there for a picnic basket; pants that a clown would refuse to wear on the grounds that they were too undignified. The young men wear these pants really low, so that the waist is about knee level and the pants butt drags on the ground. You could not be an effective criminal wearing pants like these, because you'd be unable to flee on foot with any velocity.

POLICE OFFICER: We tracked the alleged perpetrator from the crime scene by following the trail of his dragging pants butt.

PROSECUTOR: And what was he doing when you caught up with him?

POLICE OFFICER: He was hobbling in a suspicious manner.

What I want to know is, how do young people buy these pants? Do they try them on to make sure they DON'T fit? Do they take along a 570-pound friend, or a mature polar bear, and buy pants that fit HIM?

I asked my son about these pants, and he told me that mainly "bassers" wear them. "Bassers" are people who like a lot of bass in their music. They drive around in cars with four-trillion-watt sound systems playing recordings of what sound like aboveground nuclear tests, but with less of an emphasis on melody.

My son also told me that there are also people called "posers" who DRESS like "bassers," but are, in fact, secretly "preppies." He said that some "posers" also pose as "headbangers," who are people who like heavy-metal music, which is performed by skinny men with huge hair who stomp around the stage, striking their instruments and shrieking angrily, apparently because somebody has stolen all their shirts.

"Like," my son said, contemptuously, "some posers will act like they like Metallica, but they don't know anything about Metallica."

If you can imagine.

I realize I've mainly been giving my side of the parent-teenager relationship, and I promise to give my son's side, if he ever comes out of his room. Remember how the news media made a big deal about it when those people came out after spending two years inside Biosphere 2? Well, two years is nothing. Veteran parents assure me that teenagers routinely spend that long in the *bathroom*. In fact, veteran parents assure me that I haven't seen *anything* yet.

"Wait till he gets his driver's license," they say. "That's when Fred and I turned to heroin."

Yes, the next few years are going to be exciting and challenging. But I'm sure that, with love and trust and understanding, my family will get through them OK. At least *I* will, because I plan to be inside Biosphere 3.

A Uniform Image

by Miriam Rinn

At what point does individual expression become public outrage? When the high school in this play considers changing its dress code, the students struggle with difficult decisions about personal freedom and responsibility.

CHARACTERS

RICKI, *a high-school junior at George Washington High School*
JENNY, *a senior on the staff of the school paper,* The Washington Report
LENNY, *a junior and* JENNY'S *cousin*
LARRY, *a senior, who takes pictures for the school paper*
MR. SIMPSON, *an English teacher and adviser to the school paper*
MR. GRUBER, *principal*

SCENE 1

The office of The Washington Report, *a small room cluttered with papers, computer terminals, etc.* JENNY, *dressed in all black, with a lot of metallic jewelry, and wearing a backpack, wanders in. Her hair is spiked and dusted with pink spray, and she has an intelligent, attentive look. She is reading a memorandum, which she holds in her hand. In a minute or two,* RICKI, *immaculately dressed in preppy style, comes in, also holding a memo.*

JENNY: Hey, Ricki, what does this mean? [*Reading from memo*] "George Washington High School is considering a new dress code." Do you think they mean we'll have to wear uniforms? There have been rumors about that for the last month. It's on the agenda for this month's Board of Ed meeting, I've heard.

RICKI: No way. They can't mean that. I'll die if I have to wear a uniform. They probably just mean we can't wear shorts or tank tops or stuff like that.

> [RICKI *drops her backpack and she and* JENNY *stand close together and study the memo.* LARRY, *wearing urban hip-hop-style clothing with a camera slung around his neck, walks in. He also has the memo in his hands.*]

LARRY: What's up with this new dress code? You think they're talking about uniforms? They can't make me wear a uniform. I've seen some of those suckers who wear uniforms to school. They look stupid, man. They look like their mothers pick out their clothes.

> [*Suddenly there's an announcement over a loudspeaker.*]

MR. GRUBER'S VOICE: Attention, all students. This is your principal. A new dress code, which is mentioned in the memo that your teachers passed out, is under consideration. If passed by the Board, which meets next week, girls will wear white blouses and blue jumpers. Boys will wear white shirts and blue trousers. Only dark leather shoes will be permitted. No sneakers, sandals, or boots. Any student found wearing something other than this uniform will be sent home. This proposed change in policy is for your own good, and will promote a calmer learning environment in our school. Thank you.

RICKI [*wailing*]: What does he mean, for our own good? This is absolutely horrible. I won't, absolutely won't wear a dumb white blouse and some gross jumper. No way. I'll stay home from school, I'll join a convent—No, wait, they wear uniforms too. Well, there is no way I'm leaving my house wearing those clothes. People will think I'm a total loser.

LARRY: Where does the principal get off, telling us what to wear? We have a right to wear whatever we want. If I want to dress this way, that's my decision. Can't nobody tell me what to put on.

JENNY: It's unconstitutional. They're taking away our rights to be ourselves.

RICKI [*looking at Jenny*]: Well, you're the editor of the paper. Why don't you write an editorial or something?

JENNY: I intend to. The principal is still ticked off over my last editorial about cold pizza in the lunchroom, but wait until he reads the one I'm going to write.

MR. SIMPSON [*walking into office*]: I guess you heard the announcement. Believe it or not, you'll get used to wearing uniforms. In fact, it'll make life much easier. Just think of the time you'll save in the morning deciding what to wear, time you could spend—wait a minute, I've got it—reading a book, writing a poem, studying for your SATs! [MR. SIMPSON *waits momentarily for the students to laugh, and when they don't, he looks sheepish and then composes himself again.*] Seriously, uniforms save parents a lot of money and they take the emphasis off clothes. That's a good thing, especially in such a diverse school.

JENNY [*walks over to* SIMPSON]: What's going on here, Mr. Simpson? You're our adviser, you can tell us. Can they really do this? Will the Board approve it?

MR. SIMPSON: I don't see why not. Many schools have instituted a strict dress code and seen violence and other problems diminish. No more stolen sports-team jackets, no more fights over gang colors, no more muggings for hundred-dollar sneakers. Who wouldn't want that? Mr. Gruber shouldn't have too hard a time convincing the Board.

LARRY: Yeah, well, he's not going to convince *me*.

MR. SIMPSON: Uniforms are a way to bring people together, Larry, and that would be a good thing at Washington, don't you think? You can all be Washington students rather than freaks and druggies and jocks and hip-hoppers and whatever. The school needs to do something to break up all the tension around here.

LARRY: It's going to take a lot more than uniforms to make people get along. Anyway, why do we all have to get along? I like to hang with my own folks, and other people can hang with theirs. Where's the law that says we all have to be brothers?

RICKI [*looking confused*]: What are you talking about? Uniforms are ugly, and you can't even shop for them. Your mother can just order them over the phone. They are, like, the pits. I wouldn't even want to be seen with someone wearing one.

[LENNY *enters and stands to the side wearing Army fatigue pants, military-style boots, khaki T-shirt, and a chain around his neck. His hair is very short, almost shaved off. He stands quietly, listening.*]

JENNY: Forget all this! The principal and the Board of Education do not have the right to tell me what to wear. It's got to be against the law! This is still a free country, isn't it? What about our rights?

LENNY: That's where you've made your mistake, cousin. You don't have any rights. We've lost our freedom to do-gooders and bureaucrats like our esteemed principal, Mr. This-is-for-your-own-good Gruber. They tell us where we can live, how fast we can drive, what we do with our money, so why not what to wear?

JENNY [*in a tired voice*]: Oh, Lenny, don't start with that stuff again. We have a real problem here.

LENNY: You're right, we do. It's a problem that's destroying our country, and the only way to deal with it is for all right-thinking people to stand together. We're in agreement for a change, Jenny. I refuse to wear the school uniform too. I have my own clothes to wear, clothes that tell people who I am and what I believe.

SCENE 2

A corner table in the lunchroom. JENNY, RICKI, *and* LARRY *are sitting over the remains of their lunches. Occasionally, one of them calls a greeting to another student passing by.*

JENNY: Just wait till Mr. Gruber reads my editorial in Friday's paper. This is really about freedom of expression. I mean, what I wear tells the world a lot about me, about my opinions, about the music I like, about my outlook on the world. I look at you, Larry, and I know right away that you don't listen to country and western and that you identify with poor people and stuff. When I look at Ricki, I can tell her favorite TV show is "The Brady Bunch."

LARRY [*laughing*]: Whoa, she dissed you, Miss Ricki!

JENNY: No, no, I love Ricki. She's perfect. But you know what I mean. The clothes we choose to wear say a lot about us. Uniforms lump us

11

all together. It's hard enough for teenagers to find out who they are without taking their clothing choices away from them. Anyway, that's what I wrote in the editorial. I showed it to Simpson and called my sister's boyfriend too. He's in law school and he agrees that there should be some kind of free expression issue here.

RICKI [*deeply dejected*]: Oh, what's the point? No one's going to listen to us, anyway. I mean, who cares what a bunch of kids wear?

LARRY: The kids do.

JENNY: Well, I care what I wear, that's for sure. We have to stick together. If all the kids refuse to wear a uniform, how are they going to make us?

> [LENNY *comes out wearing the same clothes he wore before, except that now he has a large metal medallion with a swastika on it hanging from the chain around his neck. Walks over to the table. A few students turn to stare at him.*]

LENNY: I'm with you. We have to stick together.

LARRY: Hey, what's up with the jewelry, man? You joining the Nazi party now?

LENNY: They were great soldiers. They came this close to winning.

RICKI: That's not true. That can't be true, can it?

LENNY: How do you know? Your brain has been washed by all the propaganda you hear all day long.

LARRY: Those punks couldn't have won, and a good thing too. They weren't too fond of people who didn't look like them, you know. They were trying to make the world safe for themselves and no one else.

LENNY: What's wrong with that? Isn't that what everybody does, look out for himself?

JENNY [*impatiently*]: You're nuts, Lenny. You've been on the Internet too long. This is for real.

> [MR. SIMPSON *comes on stage. Looks at* LENNY *and seems upset. Walks toward table.*]

MR. SIMPSON: Lenny, you know you can't come to school like that. Where did you get that swastika, anyway?

LENNY: It's my grandfather's. He gave it to me and I'm not taking it off. He was a hero. Wasn't he, Jenny?

JENNY: Uh, I don't know. I guess he was. He has a lot of medals, but I hardly ever talk to him. He's just a crotchety old man.

LENNY: He's a lot more than that, and I'm wearing his medal. They can't make me take this off. Can they, Jen?

MR. SIMPSON: We certainly can. That's what a dress code is all about. That's why we need one. Don't you understand that people find that swastika deeply offensive? Your wearing it is an insult to all of us.

LENNY: Hold up there. I'm wearing a gift my grandfather gave me, something that's been passed down from generation to generation. If you don't like it, too bad. This is who I am. Go complain to the kids wearing stars and crosses and peace signs and all that junk. And I protest the policy about uniforms. We all protest. Isn't that right, Jen?

MR. SIMPSON: You're not a part of this, are you, Jenny? I hope not, because this isn't going to look good on your college application. "High-school editor defends wearing Nazi paraphernalia." That's not the sort of extra-curricular activities they're looking for in the Ivy League. And we need to talk about your editorial, too.

> [JENNY *is silent for a moment, thinking. She looks uncomfortably from* SIMPSON *to* LENNY *and back again.*]

JENNY: I don't know what I'm a part of right now.

MR. SIMPSON: This is something you have to decide—and fast. [*He turns and leaves.*]

LARRY: I got to go and take pictures of the football team. Later. [*Turns to go.*]

RICKI: Wait, I'll walk part of the way with you. [*She leaves with* LARRY.]

LENNY [*laughs*]: Looks like you're on the hot seat now. Gruber and Simpson don't like their star pupil consorting with the enemy. They'll let you go just so far and no further. Feel that leash around your neck, Jen? Getting a little tight, is it? That's just to remind you who's the boss. If you want to get out of this dump and go to some fancy college, you better play by their rules.

JENNY [*angrily*]: You know how much I want to go east to school. Why are you doing this? What's all this baloney about Grandpa the hero?

LENNY: He's okay. At least, he sees through all the junk coming from the government. I'm tired of people telling me what to think and how to feel. It's all lies—home of the brave and land of the free. Do you feel free? I don't. People like us don't get anything for free.

JENNY [*her voice softening*]: You were always a pain in the neck,

13

even when we were kids. I remember your dad grabbing you by the collar and pulling you off your chair because you were so fresh.

LENNY: Yeah, well now the only thing he grabs is another beer.

JENNY: This whole town is falling apart since the plant closed. I'm out of here soon as they hand us those diplomas.

> [*There's a moment of silence, with* JENNY *looking at* LENNY *and* LENNY *looking at the floor. Then* RICKI *comes to the door.*]

RICKI: Jenny, Mr. Gruber wants to see you, *toute suite.* He doesn't look real happy.

SCENE 3

> *Mr. Gruber's office. He and Jenny are sitting on opposite sides of a desk.*

MR. GRUBER: I'm very upset to hear that you've submitted an editorial to Mr. Simpson opposing the new dress code, Jenny. You're a leader in this school, and your opinion may sway many students. This policy has been carefully considered and it really will benefit the students of Washington High.

JENNY: I'm not certain about that, Mr. Gruber. After all—

MR. GRUBER: Washington students spend entirely too much time and energy thinking about their clothes. School is not a fashion show. It's where you're supposed to get an education. Uniforms will eliminate all that.

JENNY: But clothes really help kids figure out who they are. It's one of the few ways young people have to express themselves. That's what I tried to point out in my editorial.

MR. GRUBER: Is that so? And what exactly is it that Lenny Helfin is trying to express? His admiration for one of the 20th century's most notorious murderers? How do you think people my age feel looking at him? My uncle died fighting the Nazis. That boy is a one-man advertisement for the need for uniforms.

JENNY: Oh, Lenny's not a Nazi. He's just ticked off at the world because his father lost his job. He enjoys getting people all worked up, that's all.

MR. GRUBER: How do you know so much about him?

JENNY: He's my cousin.

MR. GRUBER: Are the two of you close?

JENNY: I guess. We kind of grew up together. Why are you asking?

MR. GRUBER: You might be the right person to convince Lenny of the value of going along with the new dress code. If he doesn't, he could be in serious trouble, you know.

JENNY: Me! He wouldn't listen to me, and I don't agree with the idea of uniforms either.

MR. GRUBER: So you've told me, but I really need your support on this, Jenny. As I said, your editorial could have an important impact on the student body. It's going to be much harder for me to support your college-scholarship applications if I believe that you can't see the value of this policy.

JENNY: What do you mean?

MR. GRUBER: Don't you know what I mean?

JENNY: Mr. Gruber, you can't—

[MR. SIMPSON *walks into the office, breathless and agitated.*]

MR. SIMPSON: We've got a problem. Lenny Helfin just got beat up pretty bad. An ambulance has been called and some teachers want to call the cops.

MR. GRUBER [*stands up*]: No, no, we don't need the police. Let's take care of this ourselves. [*Rushes out with* SIMPSON. JENNY *hurries out also.*]

SCENE 4

JENNY *rushes into the newspaper office to find* LARRY *walking out hurriedly.*

JENNY: What's going on, Larry? I heard Lenny was in a fight.

LARRY: He sure was. He got stomped by some guys from the wrestling team. You know that big guy, Mike Cohen? Well, he didn't like Lenny's jewelry and he let him know it.

JENNY: Is he hurt bad?

LARRY: I don't know, but there was blood all over his face when I saw him. They're taking him to the hospital.

JENNY: Oh, my gosh. This will just make everything worse for him. Maybe Gruber is right about the uniforms. All this fighting over clothes is crazy.

LARRY: Just because one punk wears something stupid doesn't

15

mean the whole school has to look like identical robots. Why did Gruber want to see you, anyway?

JENNY: Simpson told him about my editorial, and he wants me to change it. He says uniforms would be good for Washington High.

LARRY: Are you going to do it?

JENNY: I don't know, Larry. It seemed important when I wrote it, but now I wonder what difference it makes. Lenny's hurting, and whatever I say in my editorial won't help him. Mr. Simpson wouldn't approve it anyway. I have to get out of here, that's the one thing I'm sure about. My only chance is to get a scholarship. Why should I mess that up? Who is that going to help?

LARRY: Huh? You lost me, girl.

JENNY: Yeah, I feel that way too.

Henry the Kid, A.K.A. Billy

by Geoffrey C. Ward

Was he a misunderstood kid or a cold-blooded killer? For some reason, Billy the Kid has captured the imagination of readers since his death in 1881. Here is the true story behind one of the sad, unheroic legends of the West.

For me, the worst horror of entering a new school in the fourth grade was Show and Tell. Each morning, just after Attendance, we were expected to hone our "communication skills" by giving a little talk on something that interested us. I had no communication skills to hone—terror made me sway alarmingly and caused my voice simply to disappear when called upon (no loss, since it also prevented me from summoning up the simplest words)—and I was convinced that nothing that interested me could possibly interest my new classmates.

After several days of this, the teacher gently suggested that I might try reading something aloud. I was obsessed with the Old West then, and chose Walter Noble Burns's *Saga of Billy the Kid*, published in 1926. Burns was a veteran Chicago newspaperman, weak on research but strong on storytelling, whose protagonist was a genuine hero,

17

modest and misunderstood, an enemy of privilege and friend to the poor. Best of all, for my purposes, Burns wrote with shameless panache. Here his hero shoots his way out of a burning house: "The Kid's trigger-fingers worked with machine-gun rapidity. Fire poured from the muzzles of his 44s in continuous streaks. . . . On he ran like a darting, elusive shadow as if under mystic protection. He cleared the back wall at a leap. He bounded out of the flare of the conflagration. Darkness swallowed him at a gulp. Splashing across the Bonito, he gained the safety of the hills."

Great stuff for a 10-year-old, and my fellow 10-year-olds agreed: even the girls clapped and cheered and begged for more. For several weeks—until I reached the last gaudy page—I was a smash at Show and Tell.

If I had then been able to read aloud from Robert M. Utley's *Billy the Kid: A Short and Violent Life,* my audience's attention might have wandered some, but they would have learned a lot more about what the Old West was really like. Utley is an old-fashioned scholar in the best sense, stubbornly unwilling to rearrange evidence to fit current historical fashion: his books about the old Indian-fighting army, for example, published in the late 60s and early 70s when seldom was heard an encouraging word about the westward movement, demonstrated that neither troopers nor tribesmen ever had a monopoly on villainy—or virtue.

Unembellished facts about outlaws are hard to come by, and Utley's study is necessarily less full-scale biography than biographical sketch, but it nicely conveys the context in which the Kid's misdeeds can be understood. The Lincoln County War has been fought and refought in more than 40 films, but, as Utley wrote earlier in *High Noon in Lincoln: Violence on the Western Frontier,* the actual events failed to follow any of the "formulas favored by screenwriters. The war was not a fight between sheepmen and cowmen, or stockmen and sodbusters, or big cattlemen and little . . . , or enclosers and fence-cutters, or vigilantes and outlaws, or corporate moguls and nesters, or Anglos and Hispanics, or feuding families. . . ."

It was instead "a war without heroes," fought strictly for profit by armies of hired guns. Lincoln County sprawled over 30,000 square miles, but the only real profits to be made in this mostly empty, cashless land were government contracts for beef and other provisions with which the Mescalero Apaches and the soldiers posted nearby to keep them quiet had to be supplied. "The House," an establishment run by a hard-fisted Lincoln merchant named John J. Dolan, held a monopoly until 1876, its grip fortified by friends at court, a malleable sheriff—and a band of paid enforcers called "the Boys."

Then John H. Tunstall arrived. An ambitious Englishman with no illusions about how to get ahead in his adopted country, he wrote home that *"Everything* in New Mexico that pays at all is worked by a 'ring:' there is the 'Indian ring,' the 'army ring,' the 'political ring,' the 'legal ring' . . . the 'cattle ring,' the 'horse thieves ring,' the 'land ring,' and half a dozen other rings." In partnership with the cattle king John Chisum and others, Tunstall determined to form a ring of his own, wrest power from Dolan and his minions, and thus "get the half of every dollar that is made in the county by anyone." To back his play he hired his own gunmen, the Regulators, among them a beardless 18-year-old called "the Kid" by his mostly older companions.

His real name was Henry McCarty (William H. Bonney, the name under which he is still most often indexed, turns out to have been an alias), and he was a product of the New York slums, not the Old Frontier. His widowed mother, Mary, an Irish laundress, took him west with her at the close of the Civil War, first to Indiana, then Kansas, then to sunny New Mexico after she was diagnosed as tubercular. It was too late. She died in 1873 at Silver City. She had picked up a second husband, Bill Antrim, along the way, but once she was gone, he seems to have done little for her son other than to lend him the second of the three last names he used interchangeably.

Seeking reasons for the orphaned boy's precipitous slide into outlawry, his earliest biographers made much of his having been left too much alone at an impressionable age with the *Police Gazette.* More important, surely, was the fact that in a place where size and strength and bluster were highly prized, he was slender and softspoken and undersized—"really girlish looking," a boyhood friend recalled, with hands so small and supple they slipped easily through standard-issue handcuffs. His seems to have been an especially deadly instance of overcompensation.

Whatever its causes, he began his life of crime at 15 by stealing a tub of butter from a rancher and got caught trying to sell it in town, then stole a bundle of clothes from a Chinese laundryman, got caught again, and managed to make his escape from jail by squirreling his way up the chimney and onto the roof.

He graduated to stealing horses and rustling cattle, broke out of two more jails—part of his legend, like that of the bank robber Willie Sutton in this century, had its roots in the extraordinary difficulty the law had just holding on to him—and in 1877 at Bonito he shot and killed his first man, a blacksmith and bully who, according to an eyewitness, had once too often chosen to "throw [him] to the floor, ruffle his hair, slap his face, and humiliate him before the men in the saloon."

Utley's research shows that while he did not kill 21 men (one for each year of his truncated life, as boys of my generation fervently believed), he did account for four, and was present and firing enthusiastically when six others died. (That is not to say that he wasn't good at killing when circumstances required it: "Grant squared off at Billy," an admiring eyewitness to one of his authenticated killings recalled, "who when he heard the click whirled around and 'bang, bang, bang.' Right in the chin—could cover all of them with a half a dollar.")

The Kid's side would eventually lose the Lincoln County War: John Tunstall was murdered in the very first serious engagement, but his partners persevered and the fighting stuttered on for more than two years. There were chases, shoot-outs, and stand-offs, before the climactic five-day pitched battle along Lincoln's lone street in July of 1878 that ended with the daring escape from a burning building Walter Noble Burns described so lovingly.

In the interest of returning to some semblance of law and order, governor Lew Wallace issued a "general pardon," but specifically exempted from it the young man who now called himself Bill Bonney because he was already under indictment for murdering a sheriff. The peace that followed was only relative, in any case: after a drunken parley in Lincoln, members of both factions, glassy-eyed with whiskey and good fellowship, happened upon a one-armed attorney who unwisely refused to dance for their amusement. He was shot through the heart and left where he fell, his coat still burning from the powder flash, while all hands went off to an oyster supper. "There was really no malice in this shooting," a bystander later explained. "Life was held lightly down there in those days."

The Kid happened to have been a sober witness to the lawyer's shooting (alcohol was not among his vices), and struck with the governor what he thought was an ironclad bargain: in exchange for going through the motions of being arrested, fingering the attorney's killer, and providing information about other crimes and criminals, all charges against him were to be erased. He duly testified against others, then was told all bets were off: he would have to stand trial for murder himself. Disgusted, the Kid simply rode away from prison (thanks to a sympathetic lawman) and returned to cattle rustling.

Local stockmen, weary of their losses and with old scores to settle, helped elect a sometime bartender named Pat Garrett sheriff and sent him pounding after the Kid. On the night of July 14, 1881, Garrett shot him dead in the darkened bedroom of a ranch house in which he had taken refuge.

The first book about him was in the stores within a year. It is hard to see just what made his legend loom so large so fast. His youth had something to do with it. So did the eagerness of old allies to spin tales that reflected well on him and on their common cause. But beyond that he seems to have been genuinely amiable when he did not feel threatened. He was "happy-go-lucky all the time," a victim of his rustling admitted. "Nothing bothered him."

"You appear to take it easy," a reporter told him once, as he smiled for the crowd that had turned out to see him momentarily locked up.

"Yes," the Kid replied. "What's the use of looking on the gloomy side of everything? The laugh's on me this time."

"He done some things I can't endorse," an old friend said. "But Kid certainly had good feelings."

Wrestling to Lose

by Geof Hewitt

None of us were winners, like
Armentrout or Beebe, the heavyweight
who surprised opponents twice his size
in the Unlimited Division, flipping one
who still scowled from the peevish handshake
that had to start each match.

Spring Weekend my parents drove my date up from New Jersey
and I wrestled the 135 pounder from Peddie
who took 30 seconds to pin me Spring Weekend
the year before. My father
clapped my back in the locker room
and pronounced it "a moral victory."

Behind the gym two weeks later
the hacks on the team smoked their first cigarettes
since fall and chafed at the gung hoes
who were still running laps. Where are they now?
Well, Armentrout's big in business for sure,
and Beebe's a famous neurosurgeon!

And us hackers? I'll hazard our wages
per capita can't touch *theirs*. We were artists,
idealists, the boys who invented wrestling to lose:
slam yourself down on the mat. With shoulders flat
hold your opponent just three seconds over you
helpless in the victory pose.

The Scholarship Jacket

by Marta Salinas

Martha's grandfather is not a rich man, but he is a wise one. Can his words help to right a wrong when Martha is denied the prize she has earned?

The small Texas school that I attended carried out a tradition every year during the eighth-grade graduation: a beautiful gold and green jacket, the school colors, was awarded to the class valedictorian, the student who had maintained the highest grades for eight years. The scholarship jacket had a big gold S on the left front side and the winner's name was written in gold letters on the pocket.

My oldest sister, Rosie, had won the jacket a few years back and I fully expected to win also. I was 14 and in the eighth grade. I had been a straight A student since the first grade, and the last year I had looked forward to owning that jacket. My father was a farm laborer who couldn't earn enough money to feed eight children, so when I was six I was given to my grandparents to raise. We couldn't participate in sports at school because there were registration fees, uniform costs, and trips out of town; so even though we were quite agile and athletic, there would never be a sports school jacket for us. This one, the scholarship jacket, was our only chance.

In May, close to graduation, spring fever struck, and no one paid any attention in class; instead we stared out the windows and at each other, wanting to speed up the last few weeks of school. I despaired every time I looked in the mirror. Pencil thin, not a curve anywhere, I was called "Beanpole" and "String Bean" and I knew that's what I looked like. A flat chest, no hips, and a brain, that's what I had. That really isn't much for a 14-year-old to work with, I thought, as I absent-mindedly wandered from my history class to the gym. Another hour of sweating in basketball and displaying my toothpick legs was coming up. Then I remembered my P. E. shorts were still in a bag under my desk where I'd forgotten them. I had to walk all the way back and get them. Coach Thompson was a real bear if anyone wasn't dressed for P.E. She had said I was a good forward and once she even tried to talk Grandma into letting me join the team. Grandma, of course, said no.

I was almost back at my classroom's door when I heard angry voices and arguing. I stopped. I didn't mean to eavesdrop; I just hesitated, not knowing what to do. I needed those shorts and I was going to be late, but I didn't want to interrupt an argument between my teachers. I recognized the voices: Mr. Schmidt, my history teacher, and Mr. Boone, my math teacher. They seemed to be arguing about me. I couldn't believe it. I still remember the shock that rooted me flat against the wall as if I were trying to blend in with the graffiti written there.

"I refuse to do it! I don't care who her father is, her grades don't even begin to compare to Martha's. I won't lie or falsify records. Martha has a straight A-plus average and you know it." That was Mr. Schmidt and he sounded very angry. Mr. Boone's voice sounded calm and quiet.

"Look, Joann's father is not only on the Board, he owns the only store in town; we could say it was a close tie and—"

The pounding in my ears drowned out the rest of the words, only a word here and there filtered through. ". . . Martha is Mexican . . . resign . . . won't do it. . . ." Mr. Schmidt came rushing out, and luckily for me went down the opposite way toward the auditorium, so he didn't see me. Shaking, I waited a few minutes and then went in and grabbed my bag and fled from the room. Mr. Boone looked up when I came in but didn't say anything. To this day I don't remember if I got in trouble in P. E. for being late or how I made it through the rest of the afternoon. I went home very sad and cried into my pillow that night so Grandmother wouldn't hear me. It seemed a cruel coincidence that I had overheard that conversation.

The next day when the principal called me into his office, I knew what it would be about. He looked uncomfortable and unhappy. I decided I wasn't going to make it any easier for him so I looked him straight in the eye. He looked away and fidgeted with the papers on his desk.

"Martha," he said, "there's been a change in policy this year regarding the scholarship jacket. As you know, it has always been free." He cleared his throat and continued. "This year the Board decided to charge 15 dollars—which still won't cover the complete cost of the jacket."

I stared at him in shock and a small sound of dismay escaped my throat. I hadn't expected this. He still avoided looking in my eyes.

"So if you are unable to pay the 15 dollars for the jacket, it will be given to the next one in line."

Standing with all the dignity I could muster, I said, "I'll speak to my grandfather about it, sir, and let you know tomorrow." I cried on the walk home from the bus stop. The dirt road was a quarter of a mile from the highway, so by the time I got home, my eyes were red and puffy.

"Where's Grandpa?" I asked Grandma, looking down at the floor so she wouldn't ask me why I'd been crying. She was sewing on a quilt and didn't look up.

"I think he's out back working in the bean field."

I went outside and looked at the fields. There he was. I could see him walking between the rows, his body bent over the little plants, hoe in hand. I walked slowly out to him, trying to think how I could best ask him for the money. There was a cool breeze blowing and a sweet smell of mesquite in the air, but I didn't appreciate it. I kicked at a dirt clod. I wanted that jacket so much. It was more than just being a valedictorian and giving a little thank you speech for the jacket on graduation night. It represented eight years of hard work and expectation. I knew I had to be honest with Grandpa; it was my only chance. He saw me and looked up.

He waited for me to speak. I cleared my throat nervously and clasped my hands behind my back so he wouldn't see them shaking. "Grandpa, I have a big favor to ask you," I said in Spanish, the only language he knew. He still waited silently. I tried again. "Grandpa, this year the principal said the scholarship jacket is not going to be free. It's going to cost 15 dollars and I have to take the money in tomorrow, otherwise it'll be given to someone else." The last words came out in an eager rush. Grandpa straightened up tiredly and leaned his chin on the hoe handle. He looked out over the field that was filled with the tiny green bean plants. I waited, desperately hoping he'd say I could have the money.

He turned to me and asked quietly, "What does a scholarship jacket mean?"

I answered quickly; maybe there was a chance. "It means you've earned it by having the highest grades for eight years and that's why they're giving it to you." Too late I realized the significance of my words. Grandpa knew that I understood it was not a matter of money. It wasn't that. He went back to hoeing the weeds that sprang up between the delicate little bean plants. It was a time-consuming job; sometimes the small shoots were right next to each other. Finally he spoke again.

"Then if you pay for it, Marta, it's not a scholarship jacket, is it? Tell your principal I will not pay the 15 dollars."

I walked back to the house and locked myself in the bathroom for a long time. I was angry with Grandfather even though I knew he was right, and I was angry with the Board, whoever they were. Why did they have to change the rules just when it was my turn to win the jacket?

It was a very sad and withdrawn girl who dragged into the principal's office the next day. This time he did look me in the eyes.

"What did your grandfather say?"

I sat very straight in my chair.

"He said to tell you he won't pay the 15 dollars."

The principal muttered something I couldn't understand under his breath, and walked over to the window. He stood looking out at something outside. He looked bigger than usual when he stood up; he was a tall, gaunt man with gray hair, and I watched the back of his head while I waited for him to speak.

"Why?" he finally asked. "Your grandfather has the money. Doesn't he own a small bean farm?"

I looked at him, forcing my eyes to stay dry. "He said if I had to pay for it, then it wouldn't be a scholarship jacket," I said and stood up to leave. "I guess you'll just have to give it to Joann." I hadn't meant to say that; it had just slipped out. I was almost to the door when he stopped me.

"Martha—wait."

I turned and looked at him, waiting. What did he want now? I could feel my heart pounding. Something bitter and vile-tasting was coming up in my mouth; I was afraid I was going to be sick. I didn't need any sympathy speeches. He sighed loudly and went back to his big desk. He looked at me, biting his lip, as if thinking.

"Okay, damn it. We'll make an exception in your case. I'll tell the Board, you'll get your jacket."

I could hardly believe it. I spoke in a trembling rush. "Oh, thank you, sir!" Suddenly I felt great. I didn't know about adrenaline in those days, but I knew something was pumping through me, making me feel as tall as the sky. I wanted to yell, jump, run the mile, do something. I ran out so I could cry in the hall where there was no one to see me. At the end of the day, Mr. Schmidt winked at me and said, "I hear you're getting a scholarship jacket this year."

His face looked as happy and innocent as a baby's, but I knew better. Without answering I gave him a quick hug and ran to the bus. I cried on the walk home again, but this time because I was so happy. I couldn't wait to tell Grandpa and ran straight to the field. I joined him in the row where he was working and without saying anything I crouched down and started pulling up the weeds with my hands. Grandpa worked alongside me for a few minutes but he didn't ask what had happened. After I had a little pile of weeds between the rows, I stood up and faced him.

"The principal said he's making an exception for me, Grandpa, and I'm getting the jacket after all. That's after I told him what you said."

Grandpa didn't say anything, he just gave me a pat on the shoulder and a smile. He pulled out the crumpled red handkerchief that he always carried in his back pocket and wiped the sweat off his forehead.

"Better go see if your grandmother needs any help with supper."

I gave him a big grin. He didn't fool me. I skipped and ran back to the house whistling some silly tune.

A Letter to Eileen

by Harry Noden

In this letter, a veteran teacher advises a former student on the profession she's about to enter. Mr. Noden teaches language arts at Hudson Middle School in Hudson, Ohio.

Dear Eileen,

I was elated to learn you've decided to enter the teaching profession. Our profession needs individuals with your creativity, sense of humor, and character—individuals excited by life, in love with learning, and compassionate toward others. I hope you will find, as I have, that teaching is one of life's most exhilarating occupations.

Let me share something with you—a sampling of slices from my daily life as a teacher, so you can judge for yourself if this occupation is for you. For the last seven years I've kept a journal—jotting notes at the end of each day. I've selected a few samples which I hope will convey a little of what it means to be a teacher.

11/15/95: Matt stopped after school today. Wanted to know how the fish tank was doing. Three years ago when I had him in class, he brought a 40-gallon fish tank to school, set it up, and populated it with fish. They have been swimming there ever since. Funny how important that was to him and how such little joint ventures lead to a long friendship. Each fall as the school year begins, I smile and think of Matt as I try to find that special student to care for the tank, someone who needs to feel needed.

10/13/93: I collected a batch of portfolios today. I've been working with portfolios for five years. Still don't know how to manage these damn things. If I spend only 10 minutes reviewing each student's collection of work, it will take me over 22 hours to read everything. I can't take a mere 10 minutes to travel through someone's soul.

3/9/90: Jonas approached me today. He has been having extreme difficulty with "expository" writing. Can't seem to create a solid paragraph. Poor kid struggles and seems to rarely pick up on the simplest ideas. Jonas called me aside and asked, "Mr. N., how much longer will I have to be doing this suppository writing?"

9/27/94: Brian Holmes, a student I had four years ago, was interviewed in the local paper today about a national writing scholarship he won, enabling him to attend a summer program at Purdue. He was quoted as saying, "Two teachers influenced my writing development the most: Ms. Dunker at the high school and Mr. Noden at the middle school." Wow! Now I know what a Super Bowl victory feels like. Maybe I'm in the right profession after all.

10/14/89: I took off school to go to a funeral this afternoon. Melissa, a brilliant, bubbly personality who loved to laugh and linger after class to talk, who wrote poetry with a passion, and who a few days ago, unexpectedly, without any overt sign of depression, committed suicide. I feel numb, sad, totally empty. I'll miss her. Last night, I glanced through her portfolio. It was full of so much promise and joy. I felt puzzled and kept looking for hidden clues I might have overlooked.

11/15/93: Last night I was up until 1:00 developing a search-for-gold simulation to go with the novel *The Call of the Wild.* I knew it was going to be great, that the kids would love it! This morning as I introduced my idea, Andrea said, "Do we gotta do this?" The whole class rolled their eyeballs as though in agreement with her. It was looking dismal until about 10 minutes later when Joey Baker discovered gold near the White Horse pass. He yelled out, "Wow! I struck gold! I'm rich! This is awesome!" Suddenly "gold fever" broke out and everyone was racing in search of the best spots. By the time the bell rang even Andrea had to admit, "Not bad, Mr. N."

Teaching is filled with moments like these—some funny, some sad, some just simply bizarre. Such experiences keep me in touch with the pulse of life, its heartbreaks, and its triumphs. When I see a student struggle and succeed, I see part of the spirit that lands a man on the moon, motivates a woman to write a profound novel, or triggers a halfback to drive through the middle of the line to score.

When I see a student fail, I see a setback from which recovery offers the opportunity of greater victory. I see the undaunted spirit of people like Michelle Akers, Martin Luther King, Jr., and Anne Frank. I see hope. To me that is what teaching is all about, and that's why I enjoy being a teacher.

Perhaps, like the legendary Don Quixote, I'm a dreamer, living in a fantasy world. But I believe in teachers. I believe there is no group of people on the planet, no work force in society, that exhibits more love and caring than teachers. They care about kids—often more than some parents care. Their goals in life have nothing to do with driving a Lexus on a corporation expense account. The only accolades they expect come in the form of smiles of gratitude on the faces of their students, warm greetings of recognition at the corner grocery store, and an occasional letter of thanks from a student they had almost forgotten.

For me, teaching means helping to inspire children, helping students reach for their dreams, to build those skills that will someday make them productive, loving adults. This, I believe, is an important contribution to humanity—maybe as important as they come. I hope when you have moved near the end of your career as I have, you will see teaching the same way, as one of life's truly meaningful professions.

Mr. N.

Flash Cards

by Rita Dove

In math I was the whiz kid, keeper
of oranges and apples. *What you don't understand,*
master, my father said; the faster
I answered, the faster they came.

I could see one bud on the teacher's geranium,
one clear bee sputtering at the wet pane.
The tulip trees always dragged after heavy rain
so I tucked my head as my boots slapped home.

My father put up his feet after work
and relaxed with a highball and *The Life of Lincoln.*
After supper we drilled and I climbed the dark

before sleep, before a thin voice hissed
numbers as I spun on a wheel. I had to guess.
Ten, I kept saying, *I'm only ten.*

The Climb of a Lifetime

by the Editors of Time-Life Books

In this true account, determination and courage help a young rock climber overcome a devastating accident.

On a rare occasion when surefooted 17-year-old Hugh Herr stepped into unfamiliar terrain, it nearly killed him. As it was, Herr's life was irrevocably changed, and he discovered within himself a deep well of strength and ingenuity that has given a feeling of hope to all who hear his story.

An avid, skilled rock climber, Herr set out with a friend in January of 1982 for New Hampshire's Mount Washington, the site of some of North America's most severe weather. Although Hugh Herr possessed remarkable agility and superior skill in finding and exploiting tiny hand- and footholds on sheer rock cliffs, his experience in navigating ice and snow and surviving in bitter cold was limited.

The two climbers lost their way on the mountain, and three days passed before searchers were able to find them. Herr's feet were severely frostbitten, and when gangrene set in, doctors were forced

33

to amputate both of his legs four inches below the knee.

For months after the operation, Herr struggled with despair and anger. He was wracked with phantom pains in his absent limbs. He was tortured by the symptoms of withdrawal from the morphine doctors used to control his ferocious pain. But gradually, he came to grips with his sorrow and rage and began to imagine himself regaining his strength—and even, one day, climbing again.

Herr's physical therapists told him that with prosthetic devices he would be able to walk, drive, and possibly navigate a bicycle. Climbing, they said, was out of the question. Herr almost believed them, even though he had already been clambering around his parents' house, trying some of his old climbing moves while using only his arms. The temporary prostheses caused excruciating pain— so much that Herr found it easier to climb than to walk. With the help of his brother Tony, he spent the summer pushing himself through brutal workouts. Simultaneously, he improved his walking skills using newly fitted, less painful artificial limbs.

In the following year, Herr realized that his condition could be used to some advantage. As a rock climber, he was no longer limited by the size and shape of natural feet. Herr built prosthetic devices just for climbing, the feet shaped so they would wedge neatly into cracks and grip narrow ledges that his real feet could never have negotiated. He sought even keener challenges in New York State's Shawangunk Mountains, his favorite climbing haunt. Before long he was scaling the most technically difficult routes, feats reserved to only the most proficient climbers. In July of 1985, Herr completed a very difficult ascent in New Hampshire called Stage Fright. For him, the accomplishment marked the high point of his recovery.

Stage Fright also marked a personal turning point for Herr. Applying the same single-mindedness that he had once reserved for climbing, he graduated summa cum laude from Millersville University, near his home in Lancaster, Pennsylvania. In 1991, he entered graduate school at the Massachusetts Institute of Technology, with the goal of learning to design ways for others to overcome physical losses. "Someday," he says, "when technology is advanced enough, people will no longer be physically disabled." The young man with a problem had become a solver of other people's problems.

Three Days to See

by Helen Keller

After losing her sight and hearing to a childhood illness, Helen Keller (1880-1968) was reawakened to communication through the efforts of her teacher, Anne Sullivan. She learned to write and to speak, and throughout her life she wrote articles and books and delivered lectures concerning the lives of the blind. In this article from 1933, Keller describes what she would want to see if she regained her sight.

All of us have read thrilling stories in which the hero had only a limited and specified time to live. Sometimes it was as long as a year; sometimes as short as 24 hours. But always we were interested in discovering just how the doomed man chose to spend his last days or his last hours. I speak, of course, of free men who have a choice, not condemned criminals whose sphere of activities is strictly limited.

Such stories set us thinking, wondering what we should do under similar circumstances. What events, what experiences, what associations, should we crowd into those last hours as mortal beings? What happiness should we find in reviewing the past, what regrets?

Sometimes I have thought it would be an excellent rule to live each day as if we should die tomorrow. Such an attitude would emphasize sharply the values of life. We should live each day with a gentleness, a vigor, and a keenness of appreciation which are often lost when time stretches before us in the constant panorama of more days and months and years to come. There are those, of course, who would adopt the epicurean motto of "Eat, drink, and be merry," but most people would be chastened by the certainty of impending death.

In stories, the doomed hero is usually saved at the last minute by some stroke of fortune, but almost always his sense of values is changed. He becomes more appreciative of the meaning of life and its permanent spiritual values. It has often been noted that those who live, or have lived, in the shadow of death bring a mellow sweetness to everything they do.

Most of us, however, take life for granted. We know that one day we must die, but usually we picture that day as far in the future. When we are in buoyant health, death is all but unimaginable. We seldom think of it. The days stretch out in an endless vista. So we go about our petty tasks, hardly aware of our listless attitude toward life.

The same lethargy, I am afraid, characterizes the use of all our faculties and senses. Only the deaf appreciate hearing, only the blind realize the manifold blessings that lie in sight. Particularly does this observation apply to those who have lost sight and hearing in adult life. But those who have never suffered impairment of sight or hearing seldom make the fullest use of these blessed faculties. Their eyes and ears take in all sights and sounds hazily, without concentration and with little appreciation. It is the same old story of not being grateful for what we have until we lose it, of not being conscious of health until we are ill.

I have often thought it would be a blessing if each human being were stricken blind and deaf for a few days at some time during his early adult life. Darkness would make him more appreciative of sight; silence would teach him the joys of sound.

Now and then I have tested my seeing friends to discover what they see. Recently I was visited by a very good friend who had just returned from a long walk in the woods, and I asked her what she had observed. "Nothing in particular," she replied. I might have been incredulous had I not been accustomed to such responses, for long ago I became convinced that the seeing see little.

How was it possible, I asked myself, to walk for an hour through the woods and see nothing worthy of note? I who cannot see find hundreds of things to interest me through mere touch. I feel the delicate symmetry of a leaf. I pass my hands lovingly about the smooth skin of a silver birch, or the rough, shaggy bark of a pine. In spring I touch the branches of trees hopefully in search of a bud, the first sign of awakening Nature after her winter's sleep. I feel the delightful, velvety texture of a flower, and discover its remarkable convolutions; and something of the miracle of Nature is revealed to me. Occasionally, if I am very fortunate, I place my hand gently on a small tree and feel the happy quiver of a bird in full song. I am delighted to have the cool waters of a brook rush through my open fingers. To me a lush carpet of pine needles or spongy grass is more welcome than the most luxurious Persian rug. To me the pageant of seasons is a thrilling and unending drama, the action of which streams through my fingertips.

At times my heart cries out with longing to see all these things. If I can get so much pleasure from mere touch, how much more beauty must be revealed by sight. Yet those who have eyes apparently see little. The panorama of color and action which fills the world is taken for granted. It is human, perhaps, to appreciate little that which we have and to long for that which we have not, but it is a great pity that in the world of light the gift of sight is used only as a mere convenience rather than as a means of adding fullness to life.

If I were the president of a university I should establish a compulsory course in "How to Use Your Eyes." The professor would try to show his pupils how they could add joy to their lives by really seeing what passes unnoticed before them. He would try to awake their dormant and sluggish faculties.

Perhaps I can best illustrate by imagining what I should most like to see if I were given the use of my eyes, say, for just three days. And while I am imagining, suppose you, too, set your mind to work on the problem of how you would use your own eyes if you had only three more days to see. If with the oncoming darkness of the third night you knew that the sun would never rise for you again, how would you spend those three precious intervening days? What would you most want to let your gaze rest upon?

I, naturally, should want to see the things which have become dear to me through my years of darkness. You, too, would want to let your eyes rest long on the things that have become dear to you so that you could take the memory of them with you into the night that loomed before you.

If, by some miracle, I were granted three seeing days, to be followed by a relapse into darkness, I should divide the period into three parts.

On the first day, I should want to see the people whose kindness and gentleness and companionship have made my life worth living. First I should like to gaze long upon the face of my dear teacher, Mrs. Anne Sullivan Macy, who came to me when I was a child and opened the outer world to me. I should want not merely to see the outline of her face, so that I could cherish it in my memory, but to study that face and find in it the living evidence of the sympathetic tenderness and patience with which she accomplished the difficult task of my education. I should like to see in her eyes that strength of character which has enabled her to stand firm in the face of difficulties, and that compassion for all humanity which she has revealed to me so often.

I do not know what it is to see into the heart of a friend through that "window of the soul," the eye. I can only "see" through my fingertips the outline of a face. I can detect laughter, sorrow, and many other obvious emotions. I know my friends from the feel of their faces. But I cannot really picture their personalities by touch. I know their personalities, of course, through other means, through the thoughts they express to me, through whatever of their actions are revealed to me. But I am denied that deeper understanding of them which I am sure would come through sight of them, through watching their reactions to various expressed thoughts and circumstances, through noting the immediate and fleeting reactions of their eyes and countenance.

Friends who are near to me I know well, because through the months and years they reveal themselves to me in all their phases; but of casual friends I have only an incomplete impression, an impression gained from a handclasp, from spoken words which I take from their lips with my fingertips, or which they tap into the palm of my hand.

How much easier, how much more satisfying it is for you who can see to grasp quickly the essential qualities of another person by

38

watching the subtleties of expression, the quiver of a muscle, the flutter of a hand. But does it ever occur to you to use your sight to see into the inner nature of a friend or acquaintance? Do not most of you seeing people grasp casually the outward features of a face and let it go at that?

For instance, can you describe accurately the faces of five good friends? Some of you can, but many cannot. As an experiment, I have questioned husbands of long standing about the color of their wives' eyes, and often they express embarrassed confusion and admit that they do not know. And, incidentally, it is a chronic complaint of wives that their husbands do not notice new dresses, new hats, and changes in household arrangements.

The eyes of seeing persons soon become accustomed to the routine of their surroundings, and they actually see only the startling and spectacular. But even in viewing the most spectacular sights the eyes are lazy. Court records reveal every day how inaccurately "eye-witnesses" see. A given event will be "seen" in several different ways by as many witnesses. Some see more than others, but few see everything that is within the range of their vision.

Oh, the things that I should see if I had the power of sight for just three days!

The first day would be a busy one. I should call to me all my dear friends and look long into their faces, imprinting upon my mind the outward evidences of the beauty that is within them. I should let my eyes rest, too, on the face of a baby, so that I could catch a vision of the eager, innocent beauty which precedes the individual's consciousness of the conflicts which life develops.

And I should like to look into the loyal, trusting eyes of my dogs— the grave, canny little Scottie, Darkie, and the stalwart, understanding Great Dane, Helga, whose warm, tender, and playful friendships are so comforting to me.

On that busy first day I should also view the small simple things of my home. I want to see the warm colors in the rugs under my feet, the pictures on the walls, the intimate trifles that transform a house into a home. My eyes would rest respectfully on the books in raised type which I have read, but they would be more eagerly interested in the printed books which seeing people can read, for during the long night of my life the books I have read and those which have been read to me have built themselves into a great shining lighthouse, revealing to me the deepest channels of human life and the human spirit.

In the afternoon of that first seeing day, I should take a long walk in the woods and intoxicate my eyes on the beauties of the world of Nature, trying desperately to absorb in a few hours the vast splendor which is constantly unfolding itself to those who can see. On the way home from my woodland jaunt my path would lie near a farm so that I might see the patient horses plowing in the field (perhaps I should see only a tractor!) and the serene content of men living close to the soil. And I should pray for the glory of a colorful sunset.

When dusk had fallen, I should experience the double delight of being able to see by artificial light, which the genius of man has created to extend the power of his sight when Nature decrees darkness.

In the night of that first day of sight, I should not be able to sleep, so full would be my mind of the memories of the day.

The next day—the second day of sight—I should arise with the dawn and see the thrilling miracle by which night is transformed into day. I should behold with awe the magnificent panorama of light with which the sun awakens the sleeping earth.

This day I should devote to a hasty glimpse of the world, past and present. I should want to see the pageant of man's progress, the kaleidoscope of the ages. How can so much be compressed into one day? Through the museums, of course. Often I have visited the New York Museum of Natural History to touch with my hands many of the objects there exhibited, but I have longed to see with my eyes the condensed history of the earth and its inhabitants displayed there— animals and the races of men pictured in their native environment; gigantic carcasses of dinosaurs and mastodons which roamed the earth long before man appeared, with his tiny stature and powerful brain, to conquer the animal kingdom; realistic presentations of the processes of evolution in animals, in man, and in the implements which man has used to fashion for himself a secure home on this planet; and a thousand and one other aspects of natural history.

I wonder how many readers of this article have viewed this panorama of the face of living things as pictured in that inspiring museum. Many, of course, have not had the opportunity, but I am

sure that many who have had the opportunity have not made use
of it. There, indeed, is a place to use your eyes. You who see can
spend many fruitful days there, but I, with my imaginary three days
of sight, could only take a hasty glimpse, and pass on.

My next stop would be the Metropolitan Museum of Art, for just as
the Museum of Natural History reveals the material aspects of the
world, so does the Metropolitan show the myriad facets of the human
spirit. Throughout the history of humanity the urge to artistic expression has been almost as powerful as the urge for food, shelter, and
procreation. And here, in the vast chambers of the Metropolitan
Museum, is unfolded before me the spirit of Egypt, Greece, and
Rome, as expressed in their art. I know well through my hands
the sculptured gods and goddesses of the ancient Nile-land. I have
felt copies of Parthenon friezes, and I have sensed the rhythmic
beauty of charging Athenian warriors. Apollos and Venuses and the
Winged Victory of Samothrace are friends of my fingertips. The
gnarled, bearded features of Homer are dear to me, for he, too, knew
blindness.

My hands have lingered upon the living marble of Roman
sculpture as well as that of later generations. I have passed my hands
over a plaster cast of Michelangelo's inspiring and heroic Moses; I
have sensed the power of Rodin; I have been awed by the devoted
spirit of Gothic woodcarving. These arts which can be touched have
meaning for me, but even they were meant to be seen rather than
felt, and I can only guess at the beauty which remains hidden from
me. I can admire the simple lines of a Greek vase, but its figured
decorations are lost to me.

So on this, my second day of sight, I should try to probe into the
soul of man through his art. The things I knew through touch I
should now see. More splendid still, the whole magnificent world of
painting would be opened to me, from the Italian Primitives, with
their serene religious devotion, to the Moderns, with their feverish
visions. I should look deep into the canvases of Raphael, Leonardo da
Vinci, Titian, Rembrandt. I should want to feast my eyes upon the
warm colors of Veronese, study the mysteries of El Greco, catch a new
vision of Nature from Corot. Oh, there is so much rich meaning and
beauty in the art of the ages for you who have eyes to see!

Upon my short visit to this temple of art I should not be able to

review a fraction of that great world of art which is open to you. I
should be able to get only a superficial impression. Artists tell me that
for a deep and true appreciation of art one must educate the eye. One
must learn through experience to weigh the merits of line, of
composition, of form and color. If I had eyes, how happily would I
embark upon so fascinating a study! Yet I am told that, to many of
you who have eyes to see, the world of art is a dark night, unexplored
and unilluminated.

It would be with extreme reluctance that I should leave the
Metropolitan Museum, which contains the key to beauty—a beauty
so neglected. Seeing persons, however, do not need a Metropolitan to
find this key to beauty. The same key lies waiting in smaller museums,
and in books on the shelves of even small libraries. But naturally, in
my limited time of imaginary sight, I should choose the place where
the key unlocks the greatest treasures in the shortest time.

The evening of my second day of sight I should spend at a theater
or at the movies. Even now I often attend theatrical performances of
all sorts, but the action of the play must be spelled into my hand by
a companion. But how I should like to see with my own eyes the
fascinating figure of Hamlet, or the gusty Falstaff amid colorful
Elizabethan trappings! How I should like to follow each movement of
the graceful Hamlet, each strut of the hearty Falstaff! And since I
could see only one play, I should be confronted by a many-horned
dilemma, for there are scores of plays I should want to see. You who
have eyes can see any you like. How many of you, I wonder, when you
gaze at a play, a movie, or any spectacle, realize and give thanks for the
miracle of sight which enables you to enjoy its color, grace, and
movement?

I cannot enjoy the beauty of rhythmic movement except in a
sphere restricted to the touch of my hands. I can vision only dimly the
grace of a Pavlova, although I know something of the delight of
rhythm, for often I can sense the beat of music as it vibrates through
the floor. I can well imagine that cadenced motion must be one of the
most pleasing sights in the world. I have been able to gather
something of this by tracing with my fingers the lines in sculptured
marble; if this static grace can be so lovely, how much more acute
must be the thrill of seeing grace in motion.

One of my dearest memories is of the time when Joseph Jefferson allowed me to touch his face and hands as he went through some of the gestures and speeches of his beloved Rip Van Winkle. I was able to catch thus a meager glimpse of the world of drama, and I shall never forget the delight of that moment. But, oh, how much I must miss, and how much pleasure you seeing ones can derive from watching and hearing the interplay of speech and movement in the unfolding of a dramatic performance! If I could see only one play, I should know how to picture in my mind the action of a hundred plays which I have read or had transferred to me through the medium of the manual alphabet.

So, through the evening of my second imaginary day of sight, the great figures of dramatic literature would crowd sleep from my eyes.

The following morning, I should again greet the dawn, anxious to discover new delights, for I am sure that, for those who have eyes which really see, the dawn of each day must be a perpetually new revelation of beauty.

This, according to the terms of my imagined miracle, is to be my third and last day of sight. I shall have no time to waste in regrets or longings; there is too much to see. The first day I devoted to my friends, animate and inanimate. The second revealed to me the history of man and Nature. Today I shall spend in the workaday world of the present, amid the haunts of men going about the business of life. And where can one find so many activities and conditions of men as in New York? So the city becomes my destination.

I start from my home in the quiet little suburb of Forest Hills, Long Island. Here, surrounded by green lawns, trees, and flowers, are neat little houses, happy with the voices and movements of wives and children, havens of peaceful rest for men who toil in the city. I drive across the lacy structure of steel which spans the East River, and I get a new and startling vision of the power and ingenuity of the mind of man. Busy boats chug and scurry about the river—racy speedboats, stolid, snorting tugs. If I had long days of sight ahead, I should spend many of them watching the delightful activity upon the river.

I look ahead, and before me rise the fantastic towers of New York, a city that seems to have stepped from the pages of a fairy story. What an awe-inspiring sight, these glittering spires, these vast banks

43

of stone and steel—structures such as the gods might build for themselves! This animated picture is a part of the lives of millions of people every day. How many, I wonder, give it so much as a second glance? Very few, I fear. Their eyes are blind to this magnificent sight because it is so familiar to them.

I hurry to the top of one of those gigantic structures, the Empire State Building, for there, a short time ago, I 'saw' the city below through the eyes of my secretary. I am anxious to compare my fancy with reality. I am sure I should not be disappointed in the panorama spread out before me, for to me it would be a vision of another world.

Now I begin my rounds of the city. First, I stand at a busy corner, merely looking at people, trying by sight of them to understand something of their lives. I see smiles, and I am happy. I see serious determination, and I am proud. I see suffering, and I am compassionate.

I stroll down Fifth Avenue. I throw my eyes out of focus, so that I see no particular object but only a seething kaleidoscope of color. I am certain that the colors of women's dresses moving in a throng must be a gorgeous spectacle of which I should never tire. But perhaps if I had sight I should be like most other women—too interested in styles and the cut of individual dresses to give much attention to the splendor of color in the mass. And I am convinced, too, that I should become an inveterate window shopper, for it must be a delight to the eye to view the myriad articles of beauty on display.

From Fifth Avenue I make a tour of the city—to Park Avenue, to the slums, to factories, to parks where children play. I take a stay-at-home trip abroad by visiting the foreign quarters. Always my eyes are open wide to all the sights of both happiness and misery so that I may probe deep and add to my understanding of how people work and live. My heart is full of the images of people and things. My eye passes lightly over no single trifle; it strives to touch and hold closely each thing its gaze rests upon. Some sights are pleasant, filling the heart with happiness; but some are miserably pathetic. To these latter I do not shut my eyes, for they, too, are part of life. To close the eye on them is to close the heart and mind.

My third day of sight is drawing to an end. Perhaps there are many serious pursuits to which I should devote the few remaining hours, but I am afraid that on the evening of that last day I should again run away to the theater, to a hilariously funny play, so that I might appreciate the overtones of comedy in the human spirit.

At midnight my temporary respite from blindness would cease, and permanent night would close in on me again. Naturally in those three short days I should not have seen all I wanted to see. Only when darkness had again descended upon me should I realize how much I had left unseen. But my mind would be so crowded with glorious memories that I should have little time for regrets. Thereafter the touch of every object would bring a glowing memory of how that object looked.

Perhaps this short outline of how I should spend three days of sight does not agree with the program you would set for yourself if you knew that you were about to be stricken blind. I am, however, sure that if you actually faced that fate, your eyes would open to things you had never seen before, storing up memories for the long night ahead. You would use your eyes as never before. Everything you saw would become dear to you. Your eyes would touch and embrace every object that came within your range of vision. Then, at last, you would really see, and a new world of beauty would open itself before you.

I who am blind can give one hint to those who see—one admonition to those who would make full use of the gift of sight: use your eyes as if tomorrow you would be stricken blind. And the same method can be applied to the other senses. Hear the music of voices, the song of a bird, the mighty strains of an orchestra, as if you would be stricken deaf tomorrow. Touch each object you want to touch as if tomorrow your tactile sense would fail. Smell the perfume of flowers, taste with relish each morsel, as if tomorrow you could never smell and taste again. Make the most of every sense; glory in all the facets of pleasure and beauty which the world reveals to you through the several means of contact which Nature provides. But of all the senses, I am sure that sight must be the most delightful.

The Children's Wing

by Joyce Johnson

The inability to form friendships or connect emotionally to others may be the greatest handicap of all. This story explores the collision of such a solitary boy with the other patients he meets in a hospital ward. Nicky's mother is desperate to protect her child from any additional pain, but will she be able to do so?

The summer Nicky was so sick, I would leave work a little early and go to the Chinese takeout place on 49th Street. After a while it was my regular routine. Nicky would call me at the office and place his order. "An egg roll, of course," he'd say. "And sweet and sour shrimp. And Mom, would you bring me a Coke?" I didn't like him to have soft drinks, but he'd say, "Please, please," trying to sound pitiful, and I'd always get one for him in the end. It was hard to refuse him anything that summer. When I'd get to the hospital the other mothers would be there already with their shopping bags. Soon whole families would be gathered around the bedsides of the children, everyone eating out of foil containers or off paper plates, like an odd kind of picnic or a birthday party that had been displaced.

The children's wing was in the oldest part of the hospital, one of those gloomy gray stone buildings put up at the turn of the century.

There was a marble rotunda on the ground floor. When you took the elevator up, there was no more marble, just dim green corridors and unending linoleum and muffled fake laughter from all the television sets.

I was never in the ward when the television wasn't on. The kids must have pressed the switches the moment they woke up. If you came in the afternoon, it would be soap operas or game shows; in the evening it would be reruns of *M*A*S*H* or *The Odd Couple*. There was a volunteer who called herself The Teacher and came around with little workbooks. She told me once she was going to bring Nicky some literature to explain what a biopsy was. In a stern voice I said, "I'd much rather you didn't."

I kept thinking Nicky's time in the children's ward would irrevocably change him. A shadow was falling across his vision of life and there was nothing I could do. Once I went to talk to a psychiatrist. He said, "What can I tell you? Either this will do damage to your son, or he will rise to the occasion and be a hero." This immediately comforted me, though it's hard to say why. Somehow I could accept the logic of that answer.

Nicky had seniority in Room K by August. New little boys kept coming and going, accident cases mostly. They lay beached on those high white beds, bewildered to find themselves in arrested motion. Each had been felled by some miscalculation—running out too fast in front of a car, jumping off a fence the wrong way. They'd go home with an arm or leg in a cast and sit out the summer, listening for the bell of the ice-cream truck, driving their mothers crazy. "Hey man, what you break?" they'd ask Nicky, looking at the plaster around his torso with respect. "You break your back or something?"

He could explain his condition as if he were a junior scientist laying out an interesting problem, using the language he'd picked up from the doctors— "left lumbar vertebra . . . unknown organism." He'd say, "You see, in the X-ray there's a white swelling on the left lumbar vertebra." There were men in a laboratory hunting the unknown organism. He made it sound like a movie—you could imagine the men in their white coats bent over their test tubes. All they had to do was find it, he'd say in a confident voice, and then they could cure him.

Sometimes I'd look around the room and stare at all those simple broken limbs in envy. I wondered if Nicky did that, too. Why had it been necessary for him to learn the awful possibilities, how your own body could suddenly turn against you, become the enemy?

He was the little scientist and he was the birthday boy. When the pain would come, he'd hold on to my hand the way he had at home on those nights I'd sat up with him. "Do you see that?" he'd say, pointing to the decal of a yellow duckling on the wall near his bed. "Isn't that ridiculous to have that here, that stupid duck?"

I agreed with him about the duck and Room K's other decorations—brown Disneyesque bunnies in various poses, a fat-cheeked Mary and her little lamb, all of them scratched and violently scribbled over. I could see how they threatened the dignity of a 10-year-old. The hospital would turn you into a baby if you didn't watch out.

I kept buying Nicky things; so did his father. With a sick child, you're always trying to bring different pieces of the outside in, as if to say, *That's* the reality, not this. There was a game called Boggle that he was interested in for a week, and his own tape recorder, which fell off the bed one day and broke, and incredibly intricate miniature robots from Japan. All this stuff piled up around him. The fruit my mother brought him turned brown in unopened plastic bags.

Nicky liked only one thing, really; he could have done without all the rest. A fantasy war game called D&D that was all the rage among the fifth graders. I never even tried to understand it. I just kept buying the strange-looking dice he asked for and the small lead figures that he'd have to paint himself—dragons and wizards and goblins—and new strategy books with ever more complicated rules. "I want to live in a fantasy world," he told me. I remember it shocked me a little that he knew so explicitly what he was doing.

He refused to come back from that world very much. There were nights he'd hardly stop playing to talk to me. He'd look up only when I was leaving to tell me the colors he needed. When I'd encourage Nicky to get to know the other kids, he'd look at me wearily. "They don't have the same interests," he'd say.

"Maybe you could interest them in what you're doing."

"Mom . . . I can't. I'd have to start them from the beginning."

Still, I was grateful to the makers of D&D, grateful he had a way to lose himself. There were things happening in the children's wing I didn't want him to find out about, things I didn't want to know. If you walked those corridors you passed certain quiet, darkened rooms where there were children who weren't ever going to get well; there were parents on the elevator with swollen faces who'd never look you in the eye. A little girl in Room G died during visiting hours. I could hear her as soon as I got off on the fifth floor, a terrible high-pitched, rattling moan that I'll never forget. It went on and on and there were doctors running down the hall with machinery.

I walked into Nicky's room with my shopping bag from the Chinese takeout place. He was staring at all his figures lined up in battle formation; he didn't say hello. The other kids weren't saying much either. Their parents hadn't come yet. One little boy, looking scared, asked me, "What's that noise out there?" "Oh, someone's very sick tonight," I said, and I closed the door. I just shut the sound out. I suppose any other parent would have done the same. The strange thing was, I felt I'd done something wrong, that we all should have acknowledged it somehow, wept for the child who was dying.

I used to try to get Nicky out of bed for some exercise. We'd walk up and down outside his room very slowly, the IV apparatus trailing along on its clumsy, spindly stand like a dog on a leash. Some nights we'd sit on the brown plastic couch in the visitors' lounge, and Nicky would drink his Coke and go over his strategy books.

A mentally disturbed boy appeared there one night. He was tall and had a man's build already, muscled arms and shoulders, though I later found out he was only 15. He had a face that could have been beautiful, but you didn't want to see his eyes. They were red and inflamed, emptier than a statue's. I thought of the word *baleful* when I saw them. The boy with the baleful eyes. He was wearing dirty jeans and an old gray T-shirt. I thought he might have come in off the street.

Nicky and I were alone. This boy walked right over and stared down at us. I spoke to him softly, trying to sound calm. "Are you looking for someone?" I said.

He shook his head, grinning. "Who? Looking for Mr. Who. Have you seen Who?"

I said I hadn't seen him.

"Are you a nurse? You're not a nurse."

"The nurses are outside," I said. "Just down the hall."

He sat down next to Nicky. He rapped on Nicky's cast with his knuckles. "Hello, Mr. Who. Want a cigarette?"

Nicky was sitting very still. "No thanks. I don't smoke," he said in a small voice.

The boy laughed and stood up. He took out a pack of cigarettes and some matches. He lit a match and held it up close to Nicky's face for a moment. Then he lit his cigarette with it and stared down at us a while longer. "My name is Joseph," he said. "Do you like me?"

"I like you very much," I said.

He studied me a long time, almost as if I were someone he remembered. Then he threw the cigarette on the floor and drifted out.

Earlier that day, a boy from Nicky's room had gone home. When we got back there, we saw that the empty bed had been taken. A small suitcase stood beside it and a nurse was tucking in the blanket, making hospital corners. A little while later an intern led Joseph in, dressed in pajamas. "Mom," Nicky whispered. "They're putting him in *here*."

"Don't worry about it, honey," I told him.

I went out to the nurse on duty at the desk and made a complaint. They had no right to put a boy like that in with sick children. The children would be frightened, they had enough to contend with.

"It's the only bed available," the nurse said. "There's no private room for him now. Try to understand—he's sick, too, he needs care. We're going to watch the situation very carefully." I told her about the cigarettes and the matches. She said, "My God. We'll take care of that."

"Where does he come from, anyway?" I asked, and she told me the name of some institution upstate.

My telephone rang in the middle of the night. A nurse said, "Hold on. Your son insists on speaking to you."

Nicky got on the phone, all keyed up and out of breath. "Mom, you have to give me some advice. You know that guy Joseph?"

"What's the matter, Nick?" I said.

"Well, guess who he's picked to be his friend? He keeps getting off his bed and coming over to talk to me. It's too weird. I don't know what to say to him, so I just listen."

I wanted to go straight to the hospital and bring Nicky home. I said, "I guess you're doing the right thing, honey." I asked him if he was scared.

"Not so much. But it's hard, Mom."

"The next time he bothers you, just pretend you're asleep. Maybe he'll go to sleep, too."

"O.K.," Nicky said. "Can I call you again if I have to?"

I turned on the lights and sat up and read so I'd be sure to hear the phone. I called him back early in the morning. Joseph was sleeping, Nicky told me. The nurse had finally given him some kind of pill.

I went to the office as usual but I couldn't get much accomplished. Around three I gave up and went to the hospital. They were mopping the corridors and a game show was on in Room K. A housewife from Baltimore had just won a walk-in refrigerator and a trip for two to Bermuda. "Yah! It's the fat lady! I knew it!" a kid was yelling. I found Nicky propped up in bed painting a dragon, making each scale of its wings a different color. I looked around for Joseph, but I didn't see him.

"I'm concentrating, Mom," Nicky said.

"Is everything okay?" I whispered.

With a sigh he put down his brush. "Joseph is taking a walk. That's what Joseph does. But don't worry—he'll be back." Then he said, "Mom, sometimes Joseph seems almost all right. I ask him questions and he tells me very sad things."

"What kinds of things?"

"Stuff about his life. He doesn't go to school, you know. He lives in a hospital with grown-ups. He thinks he's going to live there a long time—maybe always."

When Nicky was little, I used to take him to nursery school on the way to work. It wasn't convenient, but I never minded. The place, as I recall it, was always yellow with sunlight. Green sweet-potato vines climbed up the windows and there were hamsters dozing in a cage. In the morning the teacher would put up the paintings the children had done the day before. You could smell crayons, soap, chalk dust. And all the little perfect children pulling off their coats had a shine about them, a newness. I was getting my divorce then. Sometimes the thought of that bright place would get me through the day, the idea that it was there and that Nicky was in it—as if I'd been allowed a small vision of harmony.

I thought of it again that afternoon at the hospital. I couldn't get back to it; it was lost, out of reach.

In the institution Joseph came from, they must have kept him very confined. In the children's wing he roamed the corridors. One day a nurse found him standing in a room he shouldn't have been in and had to bring him back to Room K. "Joseph, you stay in here," she admonished him. He walked up and down, banging his fists against the beds. He poked at little kids and chanted at the top of his voice, "Hey! Hey! What do you say today!"—which might have been a form of greeting.

He stopped by Nicky's bed and watched him paint the dragon. He pressed down on it with his thumb. "Hey, the mad monster game!"

"Wet paint, Joseph," warned Nicky.

Joseph took the dragon right off the night table. "Joseph, you creep!" Nicky yelled, his eyes filling with tears.

I went over to him and held out my hand. "I'm sorry. Nicky needs his dragon." It was odd how Joseph inspired politeness.

He stared down at my open palm as if puzzling over its significance. "That wasn't Nick's," he said.

Joseph stood by the door in the evening when the families came, when the bags of food were opened and the paper plates passed around. I went out to get Nicky a hamburger and a chocolate milkshake. When I came back, the room smelled of fried chicken and everyone was watching *The Odd Couple*. Joseph lay on his bed. He had put his arm over those red eyes, as if the light were hurting him.

Nicky tapped my arm. "Do you see that, Mom? No one came for him."

I said, "Maybe there's no one to come, Nicky."

"Someone should."

I handed him his milkshake. He peeled the paper off the straw and stuck it through the hole in the lid of the container. For a while he twirled it around. "Mom, I think you should get him something. Can you?"

I went down to the machines in the basement and got Joseph an ice-cream sandwich. I put it on his dinner tray. I said, "Joseph, this is for you." His arm stayed where it was. I touched his shoulder. "Do you like ice cream?" I said loudly.

Mrs. Rodriguez, who was sitting beside the next bed, talking to her son Emilio, whispered to me fiercely. "*Loco. Muy loco.* You understand? No good here. No good."

She wasn't wrong. I couldn't argue. The ice-cream sandwich was melting, oozing through its paper wrapping. I went back to Nicky and took him for his walk.

Later, out in the corridor, we saw Joseph. He took a swipe at Nicky's cast as we passed him and yelled after us, "Dragon Man and the Mom!" There was chocolate smeared all over his mouth.

The next day I bought an extra egg roll at the takeout place. It seemed I'd have to keep on with what I'd started, though I had no idea how much Joseph would remember. I kept thinking of him during visiting hours, lying there alone. What I really wanted was to walk into Room K and find him gone, some other arrangement made, so I could remove him from the list of everything that troubled me.

When I got to the hospital, some of the other parents were there, earlier than usual. They were standing in the corridor near the head nurse's desk. One of the mothers had her arm around Mrs. Rodriguez, who was wiping her eyes with some Kleenex. They gestured to me to join them. "The supervisor is coming to talk to us about our problem," someone said.

"What happened?" I asked Mrs. Rodriguez.

She blew her nose; it seemed hard for her to speak. "Joseph! Joseph! Who do you think?"

Joseph had somehow gotten hold of some cigarettes and matches. He had held a lighted match near Emilio's eyes. "To burn my son!" cried Mrs. Rodriguez. Emilio was only eight, a frail little boy with a broken collarbone.

I put down my shopping bag and waited with the others. When the supervisor came, I spoke up, too. Irresponsibility, negligence, lack of consideration—the words came so fluently, as if from the mouth of the kind of person I'd always distrusted, some person with very sure opinions about rightness and wrongness and what was good for society.

The supervisor already had his computer working on the situation. "Just give us an hour," he said.

In Room K an orderly had been posted to keep an eye on Joseph.

He'd made Joseph lie down on his bed. The children were subdued; they talked in murmurs. Even the television was on low, until a parent turned up the volume. There was an effort to create the atmosphere of the usual picnic.

Nicky looked wide-eyed, pale. "Did you hear what Joseph did to Emilio?"

I leaned over him and pushed the wet hair off his forehead. "Nicky, don't worry about Joseph anymore. They're going to move him in a little while to a room by himself."

I started opening containers from the Chinese takeout place, and there was the egg roll I'd meant to give Joseph. I angled my chair so that I wouldn't have to see him. It was as though life were full of nothing but intolerable choices.

"Eat something," I said to Nicky.

In a loud, dazed voice, a kid in the room was talking on the phone. "Hey, Grandma, guess who this is? I'm gonna see you soon, you bet. I'm gonna get on a plane and fly. Yeah, I'll bring my little bathing suit. Gonna see you, Grandma. Gonna see you."

"Mom," Nicky whispered. "Can you hear him?"

We were there when he left, everyone was there. Two nurses came in and walked over to him. "Joseph, it's time to get moving now," one of them said. "Let's get your personal things together."

They got him out of bed very quickly. One took his suitcase; the other had him by the arm. The orderly positioned himself in front of them. Nicky turned his face into the pillow when they started walking between the rows of beds. I was holding his hand and he kept squeezing my fingers, not letting go.

As he passed by us, Joseph broke away from the nurse. For a moment he loomed over Nicky and me. He kissed me on the top of the head. Then they took him out into the long, dim corridors.

When Nicky was 13, he said he couldn't remember much about his childhood. He wanted to, but he couldn't. The whole subject made him very angry. "What I remember," he said, "is Joseph."

Nicky got well but he got old.

Kids Taking Care of Kids

by Linda L. Creighton

*Because of social and economic changes, many
families have no adults at home during the day. Both
mothers and fathers are at work, and children are left
on their own or with siblings. In this article from* U.S.
News & World Report, *a journalist reports on the
millions of children who are left alone to guard
younger brothers and sisters every day.*

Long before morning light has dimmed the street lamp outside
her window, Pauline Britton smooths her hair one last time. She
steps into two tiny bedrooms and touches the sleep-warm
heads of her four children. Hurrying downstairs, she sips the last of
her hot tea and pulls the door shut as she leaves, the clunk of the
dead-bolt loud in the deserted street at 5 A.M.

From the bus, Pauline looks out at the broken streets and thinks
maybe, with a few more years of saving, her kids could wake up in a
house on a good street. But if she paid someone to stay with them
while she worked, she could not keep the dream alive. So, for the last
three years, 14-year-old Hope has been part-time mother to the three
younger children.

By 6:30, Pauline is at the nursing home where, for $7.10 an hour,
she spoon-feeds breakfasts and combs thinning scalps. She waits until

exactly 7 A.M. to dial home, "Hope, it's Mom. Time to get up. Breakfast is on the counter, and make sure the others wear their coats to school. Love you." At 7:20, Pauline phones again: "Just wanted to make sure you were all up. Love you." At 8:15, she dials again. No answer. Just as it should be, since the children should have left for school; a quick call to a neighbor confirms it. Now, knowing she has done all she can, Pauline must trust in Hope and God that things will be okay until she gets home.

HOME ALONE. No one knows how many American children become tiny guardians for younger brothers and sisters while parents are at work. Estimates of latchkey children range from 2 million to 15 million, or from 7 to 45 percent of all elementary school kids. A national survey in 1990 by the U.S. Department of Education found that 44 percent of 5-to-12-year-olds whose mothers were employed had no care arrangements at all. *Weekly Reader*, a children's publication, asked sixth graders about their after-school situations. Of 30,000 12-year-olds, half were home alone and almost 7,000 more were home with a sibling.

Only when disaster strikes is the issue confronted. A house fire in Detroit leaves seven tiny, huddled corpses; two brothers in Miami, on a waiting list for day care for more than a year, climb into a clothes dryer to play and are suffocated while their mother is at work. These stories stop the hearts of parents who know that the thin line between routine and tragedy is straddled by a child they have left to care for younger ones—usually because they can't afford to do otherwise.

There are many cases of parents who seem simply negligent: the Illinois couple, for example, who left their young daughters while they vacationed in Acapulco. But it is the parents struggling to balance child care and work whose stories go unnoticed. There are more than 23 million American children under 6, and an estimated 9 million need full-time care—yet only about 5 million licensed-day-care slots are available. Michelle Seligson of the School-Age Child Care Project at Wellesley College in Massachusetts estimates that as many as 10 million children need care before or after school—with slots for just 1.5 to 3 million.

Many of those who leave their kids alone are breaking the law—

one reason why the problem goes unreported. But even when it is legal, it is dangerous to make it known that children are home alone. Parents, teachers, psychiatrists, and children say this is America's big secret: that millions of children are left in charge because there is no one else.

Some researchers say children cannot handle the responsibility. Maryland psychologist Thomas Long says that most children under 13 cannot field more than one decision at a time, with sometimes devastating results. "In Washington, D.C., an eight-year-old left alone with a two-year-old brother couldn't rescue him in a fire," recounts Long. "Of course, we tell him it's not his fault, but he feels it is." And the chances that home-alone children will experience substance abuse, sexual activity, and low grades are high.

Yet almost without exception, parents say they have no choice. In many ways, Baltimore is a scale model of America's struggle with child care. The city was singled out in a 1991 survey as one of the best cities for child care in the country, based partly on the increase in the number of school-age programs. Yet of the 90,000 schoolchildren, almost half are latchkey. Most go home with a brother or sister.

Even when care programs do exist, costs can be prohibitive. Romaine Hooper, director of a program at Federal Hill Elementary, sees the results. "People struggle very hard to make the payments and they finally come in and just say, 'I can't make this anymore.' You know those kids are going to be home taking care of each other."

GUARDIAN ANGEL. Kelly* marches the little girls through the grocery store at parade-ground speed. "Don't you dare pick that up," she barks to Kassandra, five. To Kristy, seven: "Hey, do I have to tell you one more time not to ask for candy?" "Now, let's see what kind of bread is on sale today," she muses, comparing price tags. Kelly shows extensive experience at shopping. And the two children respect her seniority. She is, after all, their 10-year-old sister.

At the checkout counter, Kelly watches as the salesclerk punches in prices. "I think you made a mistake, Miss," she points out politely but firmly after a 22-cent overcharge. Still watching, she pulls Kassandra away from a beach ball display. When the final sale is tallied,

*Some of the families in this story asked not to use their last names.

Kelly carefully pulls a wadded $20 bill from her jeans and hands it over gravely. "Thank you," says the clerk, and Kelly replies, "I have change coming back."

Toting their brown bags along a busy Baltimore street, the girls stop to admire a squashed cockroach of impressive size. They hardly pause as a boy yells out a rude comment. Shooing the younger girls across an intersection, Kelly stops long enough to yell a ruder comment back, then flees for home.

Home is a collection of red-brick apartment buildings that Kelly's 28-year-old mother, Kim, desperately wants to escape. She takes temporary jobs and sells Avon products door to door on money-scarce streets. Meanwhile, she is trying to teach her children to survive. "It's more realistic to prepare my daughter for this neighborhood," says Kim. "I love my kids, and I'm trying to do right for them. Sometimes that means giving them responsibility that kids in other neighborhoods might not need."

Chewing a dirt-packed fingernail, Kelly sits in the small dust patch that is her yard and watches girls across the way play with dolls. "Sometimes, you know, I got to stay with my sisters, even though I want to run over there with those girls." She shrugs narrow shoulders. "I like being the boss. If a fire came to our house, I would go upstairs first and see if everybody was out. Then I would jump out the window and call the police."

Kelly is rarely without her tiny, worn belt pack, which contains the key to the house. "Fried chicken is my best thing I cook." she says. "I just got allowed to use the stove this year." Kelly pulls up Kassandra's falling pants. "See, I know how to cook breakfast, I can do laundry, I mop the floors." Discipline, she says, can be a problem. "If Kristy and Sandy make me mad, I have to kill them. Then I get in trouble. So I try and find things to calm myself down, like washing the dishes."

Though Kim's temporary job this summer was nearby, she has applied for a full-time job that includes free day care. "I'm afraid to hope for it," says Kim. "The reality is that I cannot afford a sitter if I work. Kelly has always taken it on herself to be a bodyguard for the two younger ones." But Kelly is still only 10. When someone produces some candy, she fights hotly for her share. A neighbor, Debra Fields, comes out to settle the dispute and chides Kelly, "Your mother has left you in charge, honey. You've got to show the little ones how to do."

Kelly can't decide whether she will be a hairdresser or a computer expert when she grows up, but she feels that she is prepared for the most difficult job. "I'm going to wait until I'm at least 18 before I have a baby," she declares, "but I sure will know how to take care of it."

When their mother gets home, the three little girls become equals again. At the end of the day they climb the stairs to the tiny room they share, Sandy and Kelly in one twin bed, Kristy in another. Above the beds hangs a painting: two children alone in the wilderness, holding hands. Behind them stands an angel, a guardian. It is Kelly's favorite picture.

HIS BROTHER'S KEEPER. With an elegant fringe of gray hair over warm, crinkly eyes, Martha Weisheit looks like the good, caring mother she is. She is also a good, smart lawyer. Before her present job in the Maryland public defender's office, she worked for the Department of Economic and Employment Development, traveling all over Maryland to decide unemployment claims. One day a woman told Martha that she had been fired after staying home with a sick child. Sobbing, the woman said how hard it was to find a foothold between motherhood and work. It took all Martha's strength to keep from putting an arm around her and saying, "I know exactly how you feel."

At the time, Martha had two small boys on their way home to an empty house. Her husband, also an attorney, could not leave work early when she was late. Martha had prepared for such a scenario, giving 11-year-old Ben a key and explicit orders for taking care of eight-year-old James. But she was deeply worried.

When her two oldest boys began school 20 years ago, Martha put herself through law school, studying at night and landing a good part-time job. But with the birth of two more sons, the demands of work and parenting took their toll. Martha's doctor prescribed less stress. "You don't give up your kids," says Martha, "so you give up your job."

She stayed home for eight years and took part-time work when the youngest went to school. But the travel and unpredictable hours presented a dilemma. The Weisheits had no family nearby; their friends were struggling with their own child care problems, and the neighborhood, filled with working mothers, held no kindly soul to watch the boys for a few hours. "It wasn't like Beaver Cleaver's neighborhood, where Mrs. Cleaver was at home baking cookies," Martha laughs.

Finally, with much trepidation, she and her husband decided to let the two younger boys stay on their own for those hours. "I know so many people do this," says Martha, "but I don't think there's a mother alive who breathes easily until she gets home." Summers, she says, were a nightmare. She enrolled the boys in a camp, but "camp doesn't last all day—or all summer." The boys burned up the phone lines to their mother's office, asking her to referee fights or permit them to go places. At times, she wondered how they would survive the week. "I would get a call and hear a tremendous commotion, a terrible fight going on," she remembers. "And what could I do? Go home?"

As the boys have grown, Martha says, they can get into more trouble: "You can't keep a 13-year-old locked up in a city house all day." Ben has broken almost every rule—the no-friends-over rule, the no-cooking rule, the call-Mom-if-you're-late rule. The only rule he has not broken is taking care of James.

If she had it to do over, Martha would make different choices. "I love my job, but sometimes I think I was a fool not to have become a college professor so I could have the summers off," she muses.

The boys are inseparable. Big-brother tough, Ben shoves his dirty hands deep inside his baggy khakis while he waits for James to catch up on the way home from skateboarding. "I was never scared being home," he says. James scrunches his freckle-spattered face into an imitation of Ben's cool scowl. "Nah," he says. "We were never scared. Except that one time—remember, Ben? We thought a robber was in the house. So we turned off all the lights and hid in the basement." Ben quickly replies. "Yeah, but then I went upstairs and checked things out, and everything was fine."

This past summer, the two spent a day at the state fair, without permission. "I went on the rides," says James enthusiastically, "and it was too many gutbusters. I started to puke. Ben was really good; he went and got me a Coke and sat with me until I felt better." Ben flushes slightly and mutters, "Nah, I didn't do much but sit there."

FIRST THINGS FIRST. Determined not to depend on welfare, as she did when her children were young, Deborah Branch has worked since her son Mark was three. Fond of TV cartoons and popsicles,

Mark was a handsome, happy child with cerebral palsy; he couldn't walk, talk, eat solid food, or take care of himself. Without specialized child care, which she could not afford on her salary as a security guard, Deborah, a single parent, had to depend on her daughter, LeChone, and her son Shannon to take care of Mark.

The first year that Deborah worked, LeChone was in seventh grade. She missed so much time from school because of Mark's frequent illnesses that she failed the grade. Now a striking 20-year-old who manages a shoe store, LeChone says her brother's needs came first: "I understood that my mother had to work, and I know that I helped her a lot. I remember one time especially; I had to stay inside with Mark, and I cried because it was my thirteenth birthday." But LeChone says that she developed an unbreakable bond with Mark. "I think you should always be responsible for your brothers and sisters," she says. "But if I have a daughter, I wouldn't put too much on her, not so much she'd miss her childhood."

Thirteen-year-old Shannon, says LeChone, had a harder time. One day last summer, he sat on his single bed, watching the night shadows move across the ceiling. If he stretched out his arm, he could reach across the narrow space to Mark's bed. He thought about the next day's lacrosse tryouts and imagined himself at play. And then, turning his head to look at Mark, he felt a stab of guilt. If he were playing lacrosse, who would be watching Mark?

So instead of trying out for lacrosse, Shannon waited on the row house stoop each afternoon for his little brother's bus. Even neighborhood toughs were touched by Mark's pure joy on catching sight of Shannon. In an adolescent mix of embarrassment and pleasure, Shannon carried Mark's wheelchair into the house. Cradling him, he climbed the stairs to change Mark's diaper, talking to him all the while: "Hey, hey, you happy or something? You have a good day at school, or what?" Then, with the practiced ease of a medical technician, Shannon hooked up a tube to Mark's belly to feed him dinner.

Turning on the TV cartoons, Shannon watched Mark's face for the familiar smile in the blue, flickering light. Telling his little brother he would be back soon, he walked downstairs and watched the boys go by on their way to lacrosse.

On November 15, Mark Branch died at Johns Hopkins Hospital after a brief illness. Shannon was with him. Mark was buried in a small white suit, in a coffin with gold trim. The funeral costs have forced Deborah to give up her phone service, but she has kept her job and says her faith will keep her going.

ANSWERED PRAYERS. Kim and Craig's dream is the American dream: Pull yourself up by your bootstraps, put yourself through college, work hard and get a good job, marry a nice person, have two children who make your heart burst with pride, and do your best by them. It is a dream they believe in.

But it does not come cheap. Kim is an office worker for the city of Baltimore, and Craig works in receiving at a nearby hospital. When they moved from a small apartment to a house for their children, Regis, ten, and Scott, five, their monthly housing costs doubled to $650. Food, car payments, and utilities left them with a two-digit bank statement.

But child care was a priority. Their first babysitter died in a diabetic coma while taking care of Regis, then a year old. Kim found a neighbor to help, "but I think all she did was put the baby in a child seat and leave her." So she asked her older sister for advice. "I realized that we were alone when we were growing up. My sister said it paid off in the long run, because she's a responsible adult and a good mother."

Still, Kim was cautious and she hired a sitter for $150 a week. But when she found out that the children were not getting the care she wanted, she and Craig reconsidered. Regis had begged to be at home after school, and she had always been mature. But could she handle herself and five-year-old Scott? After much soul-searching, Kim and Craig decided to trust Regis for the few hours after school she and Scott would be alone.

Her round face reflecting every thought, Regis talks solemnly about her responsibility to Scott and her parents. The most important task in her day is the arming of the burglar alarm, a ritual Regis has never, ever forgotten. "One time the power failed," she explains with great drama. "Well, I just went to the basement when the power came back on and fixed the circuit breaker so the alarm wouldn't bring the police."

Kim and Craig repeatedly go over the rules: Don't answer the phone except at designated times; never tell someone you're home alone; never answer the door; never let someone in. Several months ago Craig tested Regis, arriving home in the middle of the day and ringing the bell. To his dismay, she opened the door.

Regis's loving care of Scott would outshine most professional sitters'. Chasing him around the living room, she pins him down with tickles and kisses. Occasionally she will put a big-sister arm around Scott and whisper, "I love you," giggling at Scott's good-natured "Shut up."

It has been almost a year since the first time the children were alone, but Kim and Craig are still not used to the anxiety. It was especially difficult this summer, when camp ended in July and the children were alone all day for a month.

"Every time my daughter calls me unexpectedly at work, I get the shakes," says Kim. "I've taken every precaution I can think of—the alarm system, the fire escapes, strangers at the door. We've gone over and over things, but still I worry." And there are indeed some things Kim and Craig cannot control. Like Regis's dreams: She and Scott were playing in the front yard. Suddenly a man, an awful man with a mean dog, began to chase them. She ran into her house, where they would be safe. Turning, her heart seemed to stop. Scott was gone, snatched by the awful man. And she, Regis, the big sister, had not saved him.

After a family dinner of barbecued chicken and mashed potatoes, Regis and Scott playfully pinch each other on the way to baths and bedtime. While Regis chants the Lord's Prayer, Scott fidgets and snickers. But when it is his turn, in the way that comes only to five-year-olds, he recites his own prayer. "Keep me safe till morning light. Amen." Craig and Kim, hovering nearby, tuck the blankets around their children and hope all their prayers have been heard.

GOING HOME. At the end of her eight-hour shift at the nursing home, Pauline Britton straightens the sheets on Miss Wells's bed and tells her to rest well. She calls good night to the other patients. Then she rides the bus that will take her to her children.

Stepping from the bus, she hurries anxiously home. Did they get back from school? Are they safe inside? Then the door to her house swings open, and there is Hope. "Mom," she says. "Mom, don't worry. Everything is okay."

Three Poems

by Mari Evans

Where Have You Gone

Where have you gone

with your confident
walk with
your crooked smile

why did you leave
me
when you took your
laughter
and departed

are you aware that
with you
went the sun
all light
and what few stars
there were?

where have you gone
with your confident
walk your
crooked smile the
rent money
in one pocket and
my heart in another ...

The Rebel

When I
die
I'm sure
I will have a
Big Funeral . . .
Curiosity
seekers . . .
coming to see
if I
am really
Dead . . .
or just
trying to make
Trouble . . . .

Spectrum

Petulance is purple
happiness pink
ennui chartruese
and love
—I think
is blue
like midnight sometimes
or a robin's egg
sometimes

My Mother and Mitch

by Clarence Major

*How much can you tell about someone over the phone?
Enough to know the sort of person you're talking to? A
Chicago woman in the 1950s risks a great deal when
she decides to find out.*

He was just somebody who had dialed the wrong number. This is how it started and I wasn't concerned about it. Not at first. I don't even remember if I was there when he first called but I do, all these many years later, remember my mother on the phone speaking to him in her best quiet voice, trying to sound as ladylike as she knew how.

She had these different voices for talking to different people on different occasions. I could tell by my mother's proper voice that this man was somebody she wanted to make a good impression on, a man she thought she might like to know. This was back when my mother was still a young woman, divorced but still young enough to believe that she was not completely finished with men. She was a skeptic from the beginning, I knew that even then. But some part of her thought the right man might come along some day.

I don't know exactly what it was about him that attracted her though. People are too mysterious to know that well. I know that now and I must have been smart enough not to wonder too hard about it back then.

Since I remember hearing her tell him her name, she must not have given it out right off the bat when he first called. She was a city woman with a child and had developed a certain alertness to danger. One thing you didn't do was give your name to a stranger on the phone. You never knew who to trust in a city like Chicago. The place was full of crazy people and criminals.

She said, "My name is *Mrs.* Jayne Anderson." I can still hear her laying the emphasis on the Mrs. although she had been separated from my father 12 years by 1951 when this man dialed her number by accident.

Mitch Kibbs was the name he gave her. I guess he must have told her who he was the very first time, just after he apologized for calling her by mistake. I can't remember who he was trying to call. He must have told her and she must have told me but it's gone now. I think they must have talked a pretty good while that first time. The first thing that I remember about him was that he lived with his sister who was older than he. The next thing was that he was very old. He must have been 50 and to me at 15 that was deep into age. If my mother was old at 30, 50 was ancient. The other thing about him was that he was white.

They'd talked five or six times I think before he came out and said he was white but she knew it before he told her. I think he made this claim only after he started suspecting he might not be talking to another white person. But the thing was he didn't know for sure she was black. I was at home lying on the couch pretending to read a magazine when I heard her say, "I am a colored lady." Those were her words exactly. She placed her emphasis on the word *lady*.

I had never known my mother to date any white men. She would hang up from talking with him and she and I would sit at the kitchen table and she'd tell me what he'd said. They were telling each other the bits and pieces of their lives, listening to each other, feeling their way as they talked. She spoke slowly, remembering all the details. I watched her scowl and the way her eyes narrowed as she puzzled over his confessions as she told me in her own words about them.

She was especially puzzled about his reaction to her confession about being colored.

That night she looked across at me with that fearful look that was hers alone and said, "Tommy, I doubt if he will ever call back. Not after tonight. He didn't know. You know that."

Feeling grown-up because she was treating me that way, I said, "I wouldn't be so sure."

But he called back soon after that.

I was curious about her interest in this particular white man so I always listened carefully. I was a little bit scared too because I suspected he might be some kind of maniac or pervert. I had no good reason to fear such a thing except that I thought it strange that anybody could spend as much time as he and my mother did talking on the phone without any desire for human contact. She had never had a telephone relationship before and at that time all I knew about telephone relationships was that they were insane and conducted by people who probably needed to be put away. This meant that I also had the sad feeling that my mother was a bit crazy too. But more important than these fearful fantasies, I thought I was witnessing a change in my mother. It seemed important and I didn't want to misunderstand it or miss the point of it. I tried to look on the bright side which was what my mother always said I should try to do.

He certainly didn't sound dangerous. Two or three times I myself answered the phone when he called and he always said, "Hello, Tommy, this is Mitch, may I speak to your mother," and I always said, "Sure, just a minute." He never asked me how I was doing or anything like that and I never had anything special to say to him.

After he'd been calling for over a month I sort of lost interest in hearing about their talk. But she went right on telling me what he said. I was a polite boy so I listened despite the fact that I had decided that Mitch Kibbs and his ancient sister Temple Erikson were crazy but harmless. My poor mother was lonely. That was all. I had it all figured out. He wasn't an ax murderer who was going to sneak up on her one evening when she was coming home from her job at the factory and split her open from the top down. We were always hearing about things like this so I knew it wasn't impossible.

My interest would pick up occasionally. I was especially interested in what happened the first time my mother herself made the call to his house. She told me that Temple Erikson answered the phone. Mother and I were eating dinner when she started talking about Temple Erikson.

"She's a little off in the head."

I didn't say anything but it confirmed my suspicion. What surprised me was my mother's ability to recognize it. "What'd she say?"

"She rattled on about the Wild West and the Indians and having to hide in a barrel or something like that. Said the Indians were shooting arrows at them and she was just a little girl who hid in a barrel."

I thought about this. "Maybe she lived out west when she was young. You know? She must be a hundred by now. That would make her the right age."

"Oh, come on, now. What she said was she married when she was 14, married this Erikson fellow. As near as I could figure out he must have been a leather tanner but seems he also hunted fur and sold it to make a living. She never had a child."

"None of that sounds crazy." I was disappointed.

"She was talking crazy, though."

"How so?"

"She thinks the Indians are coming back to attack the house any day now. She says things like Erikson was still living, like he was just off there in the next room, taking a nap. One of the first things Mitch told me was his sister and he had moved in together after her husband died and that was 20 years ago."

"How did the husband die?"

She finished chewing her peas first. "Kicked in the head by a horse. Bled to death."

I burst out laughing because the image was so bright in my mind and I couldn't help myself. My pretty mother had a sense of humor even when she didn't mean to show it.

She chewed her peas in a ladylike manner. This was long before she lost her teeth. Sitting there across the table from her I knew I loved her and needed her and I knew she loved and needed me. I was not yet fearing that she needed me too much. She had a lot of anger in her too. Men had hurt her bad. And one day I was going to be a man.

When I laughed my mother said, "You shouldn't laugh at

misfortune, Tommy." But she had this silly grin on her face and it caused me to crack up again. I just couldn't stop. I think now I must have been a bit hysterical from the anxiety I had been living with all those weeks while she was telling me about the telephone conversations that I wanted to hear about only part of the time.

It was dark outside and I got up when I finished my dinner and went to the window and looked down on the streetlights glowing in the wet pavement. I said, "I bet he's out there right now, hiding in the shadows, watching our window."

"Who?" Her eyes grew large. She was easily frightened. I knew this and I was being devilish and deliberately trying to scare her.

"You know, Mister Kibbs."

She looked relieved. "No he's not. He's not like that. He's a little strange but not a pervert."

"How'd you know?"

By the look she gave me I knew now that I had thrown doubt into her and she wasn't handling it well. She didn't try to answer me. She finished her small, dry pork chop and the last of her bright green peas and reached over and took up my plate and sat it inside of her own.

She took the dishes to the sink, turned on the hot and cold water so that warm water gushed out of the single faucet, causing the pipe to clang, and started washing the dishes. "You have a vivid imagination," was all she said.

I grabbed the dishcloth and started drying the first plate she placed in the rack. "Even so, you don't know this man. You never even seen him. Aren't you curious about what he looks like?"

"I know what he looks like."

"How?"

"He sent me a picture of himself and one of Temple."

I gave her a look. She had been holding out on me. I knew he was crazy now. Was he so ugly she hadn't wanted me to see the picture? I asked if I could see it.

She dried her hands on the cloth I was holding, then took her cigarettes out of her dress pocket and knocked one from the pack and stuck it between her thin pale lips. I watched her light it and fan smoke and squint her eyes. She said, "You have to promise not to laugh."

That did it. I started laughing again and couldn't stop. Then she started laughing too because I was bent double, standing there at the sink, with this image of some old guy who looked like the Creeper in my mind. But I knew she couldn't read my mind so she had to be laughing at me laughing. She was still young enough to be silly with me like a kid.

Then she brought out two pictures, one of him and the other one of his sister. She put them down side by side on the table. "Make sure your hands are dry."

I took off my glasses and bent down to the one of the man first so I could see up close as I stood there wiping my hands on the dishcloth. It was one of those studio pictures where somebody had posed him in a three-quarter view. He had his unruly hair and eyebrows pasted down and you could tell he was fresh out of the bath and his white shirt was starched hard. He was holding his scrubbed face with effort toward where the photographer told him to look which was too much in the direction of the best light. He was frowning with discomfort beneath the forced smile. There was something else. It was something like defeat or simple tiredness in his pose and you could see it best in the heavy lids of his large blank eyes. He looked out of that face at the world with what remained of his self-confidence and trust in the world. His shaggy presence said that it was all worthwhile and maybe even in some ways he would not ever understand also important. I understood all of that even then but would never have been able to put my reading of him into words like these.

Then I looked at the woman. She was an old hawk. Her skin was badly wrinkled like the skin of ancient Indians I'd seen in photographs and the westerns. There was something like a smile coming out of her face but it had come out sort of sideways and made her look silly. But the main thing about her was that she looked very mean. But on second thought, to give her the benefit of the doubt, I can say that it might have been just plain hardness from having had a hard life. She was wearing a black iron-stiff dress buttoned up to her dickey which was ironically dainty and tight around her goose neck.

All I said was, "They're *so* old." I don't know what else I thought as I looked up at my mother who was leaning over my shoulder at the pictures too, as though she'd never seen them before, as though she was trying to see them through my eyes.

71

"You're too young, Tommy. Everybody's old to you. They're not so old. He looks lonely, to me."

I looked at him again and thought I saw what she meant.

I put the dishes away and she took the photographs back and we didn't talk any more that night about Mitch and Temple. We watched our black-and-white television screen which showed us Red Skelton acting like a fool.

Before it was over, I fell asleep on the couch and my mother woke me up when she turned off the television. "You should go to bed."

I stood up and stretched. "I have a science paper to write."

"Get up early and write it," she said, putting out her cigarette.

He wants me to meet him someplace," my mother said. She had just finished talking with him and was standing by the telephone. It was close to dinner time. I'd been home from school since 3:30 and she'd been in from work by then for a good hour. She'd just hung up from the shortest conversation she'd ever had with him.

I'd wondered why they never wanted to meet, then I stopped wondering and felt glad they hadn't. Now I was afraid, afraid for her, for myself, for the poor old man in the picture. Why did we have to go through with this crazy thing?

"I told him I needed to talk with you about it first," she said. "I told him I'd call him back."

I was standing there in front of her looking at her. She was a scared little girl with wild eyes dancing in her head, unable to make up her own mind. I sensed her fear. I resented her for the mess she had gotten herself in. I also resented her for needing my consent. I knew she wanted me to say go, go to him, meet him somewhere. I could tell. She was too curious not to want to go. I suddenly thought that he might be a millionaire and that she would marry the old coot and he'd die and leave her his fortune. But there was the sister. She was in the way, and from the looks of her she would pass herself off as one of the living for at least another 100 years or so. So I gave up that fantasy.

"Well, why don't you tell him you'll meet him at the hamburger cafe on Wentworth? We can eat dinner there."

"We?"

"Sure. I'll just sit at the counter like I don't know you. But I gotta be there to protect you."

"I see."

"Then you can walk in alone. I'll already be there eating a cheeseburger and fries. He'll come in and see you waiting for him alone at a table."

"No, I'll sit at the counter too," she said.

"Okay. You sit at the counter too."

"What time should I tell him?"

I looked at my Timex. It was six. I knew they lived on the West Side and that meant it would take him at least an hour by bus and a half hour by car. He probably didn't have a car. I was hungry though and had already set my mind on eating a cheeseburger rather than macaroni and cheese out of the box.

"Tell him 7:30."

"Okay."

I went to my room. I didn't want to hear her talking to him in her soft whispering voice. I'd stopped listening some time before. I looked at the notes for homework and felt sick in the stomach at the thought of having to write that science paper.

A few minutes later my mother came in and said, "Okay. It's all set." She sat down on the side of my bed and folded her bony pale hands in her lap. "What should I wear?"

"Wear your green dress and the brown shoes."

"You like that dress, don't you."

"I like that one and the black one with the yellow at the top. It's classical."

"You mean classy."

"Whatever I mean." I felt really grown that night.

"Here, Tommy, take this." She handed me five dollars which she'd been hiding in the palm of her right hand. "Don't spend it all. Buy the burger out of it and the rest is just to have. If you spend it all in the hamburger place I'm going to deduct it from your allowance next week."

When I got there I changed my mind about the counter. I took a table by myself.

I was eating my cheeseburger and watching the revolving door.

73

The cafe was noisy with shouts, cackling, giggles, and verbal warfare. The waitress, Miss Azibo, was in a bad mood. She'd set my hamburger plate down like it was burning her hand.

I kept my eye on the door. Every time somebody came in I looked up, every time somebody left I looked up. I finished my cheeseburger even before my mother got there, and, ignoring her warning, I ordered another and another Coca-Cola to go with it. I figured I could eat two or three burgers and still have most of the five left.

Then my mother came in like a bright light into a dingy room. I think she must have been the most beautiful woman who ever entered that place and it was her first time coming in there. She had always been something of a snob and did not believe in places like this. I knew she'd agreed to meet Mister Kibbs here just because she believed in my right to the cheeseburger and this place had the best in the neighborhood.

I watched her walk ladylike to the counter and ease herself up on the stool and sit there with her back arched. People in that place didn't walk and sit like that. She was acting classy and everybody turned to look at her. I looked around at the faces and a lot of the women had these real mean sneering looks.

She didn't know any of these people and they didn't know her. Some of them may have known her by sight, and me too but that was about all the contact we had with this part of the neighborhood. Besides, we hardly ever ate out. When we did we usually ate Chinese or at the rib place.

I sipped my Coke and watched Miss Azibo place a cup of coffee before my mother on the counter. She was a coffee freak. Always was. All day long. Long into the night. Cigarettes and coffee in a continuous cycle. I grew up with her that way. The harsh smells are still in my memory. When she picked up the cup with a dainty finger sticking out just so, I heard a big fat woman at a table in front of mine say to the fat woman with her that my mother was a snooty witch. The other woman said, "Yeah. She must think she's white. What she doing in here anyway?"

Mitch Kibbs came in about twenty minutes after my mother and I watched him stop and stand just inside the revolving doors. He stood to the side. He looked a lot younger than in the picture. He was stooped a bit though and he wasn't dressed like a millionaire which disappointed me. But he was clean. He was wearing a necktie and a clean white shirt and a suit that looked like it was two hundred years old but one no doubt made of the best wool. Although it was fall he looked overdressed for the season. He looked like a man who hadn't been out in daylight in a long while. He was nervous, and I could tell. Everybody was looking at him. Rarely did white people come in here.

Then he went to my mother like he knew she had to be the person he'd come to see. He sat himself up on the stool beside her and leaned forward with his elbows on the counter and looked in her face.

She looked back in that timid way of hers. But she wasn't timid. It was an act and part of her ladylike posture. She used it when she needed it.

They talked and talked. I sat there eating cheeseburgers and protecting her till I spent the whole five dollars. Even as I ran out of money I knew she would forgive me. She had always forgiven me on special occasions. This was one for sure.

She never told me what they talked about in the cafe and I never asked but everything that happened after that meeting went toward the finishing off of the affair my mother was having with Mitch Kibbs. He called her later that night. I was in my room reading when the phone rang and I could hear her speaking to him in that ladylike way—not the way she talked to me. It was different. She didn't need to impress me. I was her son. But I couldn't hear what she was saying and didn't want to.

Mister Kibbs called the next evening too. But eventually the calls were fewer and fewer till he no longer called.

My mother and I went on living the way we always had, she working long hours at the factory and me going to school. She was not a happy woman but I thought she was pretty brave. Every once in a while she got invited somewhere, to some wedding or out on a date with a man. She always tried on two or three different dresses, turning herself around and around before the mirror, asking me how she looked, making me select the dress she would wear. Most often though she went nowhere. After dinner we sat together at the kitchen table, she drinking coffee and smoking her eternal cigarettes. She gave me my first can of beer one night when she herself felt like having one. It tasted awful and I didn't touch the stuff for years after that.

About a day or two after the meeting in the hamburger cafe I remember coming to a conclusion about my mother. I learned for the first time that she did not always know what she was doing. It struck me that she was as helpless as I sometimes felt when confronted with a math or science problem or a problem about sex and girls and growing up and life in general. She didn't know everything. And that made me feel closer to her despite the fear it caused. She was there to protect me, I thought. But there she was, just finding her way, step by step, like me. It was something wonderful anyway.

August Afternoon

by Nancy Remaly

I remember the August afternoon
we washed the seats
in the '66 bug
with buckets of water, soap, and brushes.
Feeling a little like Cinderella
I crawled in on my hands and knees
and started to scrub
while soapy dirt ran
down my arms and legs
and sweat dripped off my hair.
I threw water on you
and in return I got
a dripping wet cloth in my face:
the battle was on.
Grimy grey water splashed over us
as we chased each other
with sponges and brushes.
We went back to work
drenched and laughing
only to emerge an hour later
looking old and prunish.
Then, like Jack and Jill
we carried our buckets
back to the house
and on the way
you said thanks
I love you.

The Last Leaf

by Julia Remine Piggin
Based on a story by O. Henry

In the days before antibiotics, pneumonia was a dangerous illness. For a poor young artist in New York City's Greenwich Village, maybe the cure was clinging to a vine.

CHARACTERS

JOANNA, *always called* JOHNSY, *a young artist*
SUE, JOHNSY'S *roommate, another artist, who is stronger and more practical*
TOR, SUE'S *boyfriend*
DR. TOMPKINS
BEHRMAN, *an elderly, bearded artist, who speaks with a European accent*

SCENE 1

A small apartment on the top floor of a building in Greenwich Village, the artists' colony of New York City, in November, 1899. It is clear that the apartment is occupied by people who have very little money but who like bright colors, plants, and art. The main room is an artist's studio, with canvasses on easels, tables holding palettes and paintbrushes, and brightly covered furniture. At one end is a kitchen; at the other, a small bedroom with a window that looks out on the brick wall of the building next door. A second window, in the studio, faces the same way.

JOHNSY *is trying to paint in the studio. She looks pale and ill. She gets dizzy and has to set down her brush and palette. Offstage voices are heard, growing gradually louder as* TOR *and* SUE *climb the stairs.*

TOR: How high up is this place, anyway?

SUE: Who cares? It's got a skylight—it's got to be under the roof.

TOR: That's wonderful, but when do we get there?

SUE: It's only three flights. Here we are! *[The door opens and* SUE *and* TOR *step into the studio.]* Isn't it wonderful? Look at that light! Johnsy's going to be a great artist. And I've already got a contract to illustrate a story about the West for *Lippincott's Magazine.* Oh, Johnsy, there you are. Here's Tor. He's here for dinner. We invited him, remember?

JOHNSY [*her voice is weak*]: Yes, I know.

SUE [*going to her*]: Johnsy, are you all right? [*Puts her hand on* JOHNSY'S *forehead.*] You're burning up. Tor, they say pneumonia is going around the Village. She needs a doctor.

TOR: Is there a doctor in the neighborhood? I'll go get him.

SUE: Yes, right across Washington Square. One of those brick houses with the white steps. I think his name is Tompkins. You'll see the sign.

TOR: I'll be back as soon as I can. [*He leaves.*]

JOHNSY: Sue, I've ruined your plans. I'm so sorry.

SUE: Never mind that. Tor understands. Let me help you into bed and make you something hot to drink. [*She helps* JOHNSY *to her feet, and half carries her into the bedroom.*]

SCENE 2

Three days later. Johnsy is in bed, a pillow under her head. Dr. Tompkins is taking a thermometer out of Johnsy's mouth. Sue stands nearby.

DOCTOR [*looking at the thermometer*]: Hmmmm. Not very good, Miss Johnsy. Sue, can I see you for a moment?

SUE: Of course, Doctor. [*They step out into the studio.*]

DOCTOR: She's not showing any improvement. Pneumonia's tricky. A lot of things can influence a patient. I hate to say it, but I think she has only one chance in 10 of getting over this.

SUE: Oh, no! She's from California, Doctor. She's never lived in cold weather before. I'm from Maine, so I'm used to it. But Johnsy—

DOCTOR: It's not just the weather, Sue. She's made up her mind not to get well. She doesn't seem to want to live. Do you know any reason why? Is there anything on her mind?

SUE: She wanted to be a great painter—to paint the Bay of Naples some day. But she's been slow getting started. Maybe she thinks it will never happen.

DOCTOR: Oh, painting. What's that? Will it buy wood for your fireplace? How about a man? Anybody she's interested in—who doesn't return her interest? How about that young man of yours? Could she be jealous?

SUE: No, no, Doctor, she doesn't even know Tor. There was somebody back in Sacramento who wanted to marry her, but she wasn't in love with him. She wanted to come to Greenwich Village and be an artist. So did I. We met in a restaurant, and decided to find a studio together.

DOCTOR: Too bad. Looking forward to a wedding gown might give her some resistance. I'll do all that medicine can do, but when a patient begins to count the carriages in her funeral procession, I subtract 50 per cent from the value of any prescription I know of. If you could get her to ask one question about the new winter styles, I'd give you a one in five chance instead of one in 10.

SUE: Oh, Doctor. [*She begins to cry. The doctor pats her hand.*]

DOCTOR: Don't give up hope. I'll see you tomorrow morning. [*He goes to the door, leaves.*]

SUE: Oh, Johnsy.

[*She cries for a moment, then brushes the tears away, straightens her shoulders, and marches into the bedroom.* JOHNSY *lies back on her pillow, looking out the window.* SUE *sits down beside her, takes a sketchpad from the night table, and begins a pencil drawing for her magazine story.* JOHNSY *makes a low sound. Her voice is very weak.*]

JOHNSY: Twelve. Eleven. Ten. Nine. Eight and seven.

SUE: What are you counting? [*She looks out the window.*] There's nothing out there but that brick wall and that half-dead old ivy vine.

JOHNSY: Six. They're falling faster now. Three days ago there were almost a hundred. It made my head ache to count them. But now it's easy. See? There goes another one. There are only five left now.

SUE: Five what, Johnsy? What are you counting?

JOHNSY: Leaves. On the ivy vine. When the last one falls, I must go, too.

SUE: Oh, no, Johnsy.

JOHNSY: I've known that for three days. Didn't the doctor tell you?

SUE: Of course not. That's silly. What have old ivy leaves got to do with you? You used to love that vine, and now you're saying it's going to make you—Johnsy, the doctor told me this morning that your chances of getting well were—10 to one. That's almost as good a chance as we have in New York when we ride the streetcars. Or walk past a building that's going up. Come on now, let me make you some hot soup. And then I can get back to work so the editor will pay me. And then I can buy my patient some port wine and myself some pork chops.

JOHNSY: I won't need any more to eat or drink, Sue. Look, there goes another leaf. That leaves four. I want to see the last one fall before it gets dark. Then I'll go, too.

SUE: Johnsy, will you promise me something?

JOHNSY: Yes, if it's something I have time for.

SUE: Johnsy, will you promise me to keep your eyes closed until I finish working? I have to hand these drawings in tomorrow. I need the light or I'd pull the shade down.

JOHNSY: Couldn't you work in the other room?

SUE: I'd rather work here near you. And anyway, I don't want you to keep looking at those silly leaves.

JOHNSY [*leaning back and closing her eyes*]: Tell me as soon as you're done. I want to see the last leaf fall. Sue, I'm tired of waiting. I'm tired of thinking. I want to go sailing down, down, down, just like one of those poor tired leaves.

SUE: Johnsy, please, try to sleep. I have to go downstairs and get Behrman up here to be my model for the old hermit miner in the story.

JOHNSY: Who is Behrman?

SUE: You know Behrman, Johnsy. The painter who lives on the ground floor. The one who's been trying to paint a masterpiece for 40 years and still keeps talking about it. He's our friend, Johnsy. The old man with the white beard. You know him.

JOHNSY: I don't want to know anybody. I want to break all my ties. All the ties that hold me to the earth.

SUE: Oh, Johnsy! Look, please go to sleep. I'll be right back. [*She hesitates, then rushes out.*]

SCENE 3

Behrman's cluttered studio. An easel with a blank canvas on it stands in one corner. Behrman sits nodding in a chair. Sue pounds on the door.

SUE [*outside, calling and pounding*]: Mr. Behrman! Please, I have to see you! [*She bangs on the door again.*]

BEHRMAN [*rising stiffly*]: All right, all right, keep your hairnet on, I'm coming. [*He shuffles to the door and opens it.*] Sue, my love! Come on in, sweetheart. Forgive me, I sipped a bit of cheer to get myself ready to start painting my masterpiece. What is it, pretty doll? Something's the matter?

SUE: It's Johnsy. You know she has pneumonia. The doctor says she doesn't want to live. She says she'll die when the last leaf falls off that old ivy vine. She will, Mr. Behrman. She really will. She's like a leaf herself.

BEHRMAN [*shouting*]: That's crazy! It's idiotic! People die because leaves drop off a vine! People are that much fools? I never heard of such stupid stuff!

SUE: I told her you'd come upstairs and model for me. I need to paint a hermit with a beard—and I need somebody else up there.

BEHRMAN: Well, I won't come! Why do you let her get such silly business in her brain? Poor little Miss Yohnsy. What's happening to her?

SUE: It's the fever. It's made her hopeless. Her mind is full of strange ideas. You're horrible, Mr. Behrman—you're mean. You don't have to pose for me if you don't want to, but you're just an old—bear! You're a silly, shallow old man!

BEHRMAN: Who said I wouldn't come up and pose? I've been trying to get a word in edgewise to tell you I'll pose! Go on. I'll follow you. Maybe I can talk some sense into little Miss Yohnsy. This is no place to be sick. When I paint my masterpiece, I'll take us all away from here. Let's go!

SCENE 4

SUE *and* BEHRMAN *enter the apartment.* BEHRMAN *goes to the window at the end of the studio.*

BEHRMAN: Look at that sleet coming down. I'm glad your studio's in the building. It must be freezing out there.

SUE: Let me look in on Johnsy. [*She goes into the bedroom.* JOHNSY *is sleeping.* SUE *pulls down the shade, goes back into the studio.*] Thank heaven she's asleep. Do you see the vine?

BEHRMAN: Yes. That leaf is still there. Just one. Looks half dead, but it's hanging on. Where do you want me to sit?

SUE: Over here. [*She goes to an overturned bucket under the skylight.*] This bucket is supposed to be a rock, outside your mine in the West.

BEHRMAN: Instead of painting my masterpiece, I turn into a cowboy sitting on an upside-down pail. Life! [SUE *begins to sketch him.*] You know, I don't think that leaf will last the night.

SUE: No, I don't either. Please, tilt your head to the left a little—that's it. You're perfect for a hermit miner.

BEHRMAN: Perfect, what's perfect? Miss Sue, I got to get back downstairs. I just thought of something I've got to do. [*Gets up and starts for the door.*] Look, you take care of Miss Yohnsy. Keep that shade down. Maybe I'll come up and see you tomorrow.

SUE: Please, Mr. Behrman, please stay.

BEHRMAN: I can't, sweetheart. Good night. [*He hurries out the door.*]

SUE: Oh, no. [*She sits down on the sofa and leans back.*] I'm so tired. So tired. [*She begins to fall asleep.*]

SCENE 5

The next morning. SUE *is still dressed, slumped on the sofa. She stirs, starts, and wakes up, bewildered.*

SUE: Where am I—it's morning. [*She jumps up.*] Johnsy! I fell asleep. The leaf!

> [*She rushes into the bedroom.* JOHNSY *is awake, staring at the drawn shade.*]

JOHNSY: Pull up the shade, Sue. I want to see.

> [SUE *hesitates, but obeys.*]

SUE: It was a stormy night, Johnsy, a lot of snow and wind.

JOHNSY: Look. It's still there. I heard the wind howling and was sure the leaf would fall during the night. But it didn't. It will today, though. It will fall today and when it does, I will die.

SUE: Johnsy, don't say that. Think of me. What would I do without you?

JOHNSY: I have a journey to make. I'll watch the leaf until it's time.

SUE: No, you won't. [*She pulls down the shade.*] I'll be in the studio, working. And you can't go anywhere.

JOHNSY: Yes, I can, Sue. The cold wind is waiting to blow me away.

SUE: No! [*She rushes out into the studio.*]

SCENE 6

> *The next morning.* SUE *has been sleeping on the sofa, this time with a blanket and pillow. She gets up and goes to the window at the end of the room.*

SUE [*amazed*]: It's still there. It's still there on the vine! [*She hurries into the bedroom and pulls up the shade.*] Johnsy! Johnsy, are you awake? Look. Look out the window!

JOHNSY: I see it. It's there. There was more rain and wind last night, but it lasted. It had the strength to live.

SUE: Honey, let me get you some chicken broth.

JOHNSY: Yes, please, I'm hungry. But first, fix some pillows around me. I want to sit up. And will you bring me a mirror? And a comb? My hair must be a mess.

SUE [*takes a mirror and comb from the dresser and hands them to* JOHNSY]: Honey, I'm so glad. [*She props* JOHNSY *up on the pillows, as* JOHNSY *starts to arrange her hair.*] I'll go make that broth.

JOHNSY: Sue, something made that leaf stay there to show me how wrong I was. It's not right to want to die. Not when you're young and there are things you want to do. I'm going to paint the Bay of Naples some day—better than it's ever been painted before.

[*There is a knock at the door.*]

SUE: That's the doctor. He said he'd be early today.

[*She goes to the door and opens it. The doctor steps in.*]

DOCTOR: Good morning, Sue. How's our patient?

SUE: Go and see, Doctor.

[*The doctor goes to the bedroom and* SUE *goes to the kitchen.*]

JOHNSY: Good morning, Dr. Tompkins. Isn't it a lovely day?

DOCTOR [*surprised*]: Well, you seem to have a new lease on life. Let's listen to that chest. [*He takes a stethoscope out of his bag and listens.*] A lot better. Good girl! [*He takes out a thermometer, puts it in* JOHNSY's *mouth.*] Just keep your mouth closed for a few minutes. I'll be right back. [*He goes to the kitchen, where* SUE *stands at the stove.*] Sue, this is an amazing change. No question, she's going to make it. Keep up the good nutrition and nursing. We've won!

SUE: Thank you, doctor. I'm so glad.

DOCTOR: Too bad about my other patient in this building, though. I'm going to the hospital to sign his death certificate.

SUE: Who is that?

DOCTOR: Old man with a beard, an artist they say. Name of Behrman. The janitor found him yesterday morning, lying in the hall downstairs. His shoes and clothes were soaked through, and he had a very good start on pneumonia. Been out in the storm, nobody can imagine why. There was a lantern, still lighted, on the floor beside him, and a ladder, and some paintbrushes.

SUE [*realizing something*]: And a palette—with green and yellow paint mixed on it?

DOCTOR: That's right. Did you already hear about it? He was still breathing when they found him, but he died today at the hospital. At his age, you don't beat pneumonia, especially when you've gone out and got yourself drenched and half frozen. But your friend is going to be up and about in no time. [*He walks back to the bedroom, takes the thermometer out of* JOHNSY's *mouth, and reads it.*] Good. Very, very good. [*SUE comes in.*] Keep up the fine work, both of you. I've got to run. See you day after tomorrow. [*He rushes out.*]

SUE [*standing for a moment, then going up to the bed*]: Johnsy, I have something to tell you. Something sad.

JOHNSY: What, Sue?

SUE: Mr. Behrman. Remember him?

JOHNSY: Oh course I do. He's our friend.

SUE: Maybe our best friend. He's dead, Johnsy. He died of pneumonia.

JOHNSY: Oh, Sue, I'm so sorry.

SUE: He wanted you to live so much. And now you have all the time in the world because of him.

JOHNSY: I don't understand. How can it be because of Mr. Behrman?

SUE: Look out the window at that last ivy leaf. Don't you wonder why it doesn't flutter or move in the wind?

JOHNSY: I guess it doesn't. That's odd, isn't it? Yes, I do wonder why.

SUE: Johnsy, that leaf is Behrman's masterpiece. He went out in the storm and painted it the night the last leaf fell.

Caged Bird

by Maya Angelou

A free bird leaps
on the back of the wind
and floats downstream
till the current ends
and dips his wing
in the orange sun rays
and dares to claim the sky.

But a bird that stalks
down his narrow cage
can seldom see through
his bars of rage
his wings are clipped and
his feet are tied
so he opens his throat to sing.

The caged bird sings
with a fearful trill
of things unknown
but longed for still
and his tune is heard
on the distant hill
for the caged bird
sings of freedom.

The free bird thinks of another
  breeze
and the trade winds soft through
  the sighing trees
and the fat worms waiting on a
  dawn-bright lawn
and he names the sky his own.

But a caged bird stands on the
  grave of dreams
his shadow shouts on a nightmare scream
his wings are clipped and his feet
  are tied
so he opens his throat to sing.

The caged bird sings
with a fearful trill
of things unknown
but longed for still
and his tune is heard
on the distant hill
for the caged bird
sings of freedom.

The Man Who Almost Married a Witch

by Julius Lester

Witches are important in folklore all over the world. They are often sinister figures with magical powers. This African-American tale, drawn from the Uncle Remus stories, humorously relates how a man avoids a hideous fate.

I don't know whether there are witches going around today. Seems to me that all the electricity and neon lights and waves from the TVs and radios would make it mighty hard for a witch to know night from day. If I was you, I wouldn't be worried about witches. I'd just enjoy the stories and leave it at that.

Long, long time ago, when the moon was a whole lot bigger than it is now, there was a Witch-Wolf that lived way back in the swamp where the alligators and snakes laid around in the moonshine, flossing each other's teeth.

This Witch-Wolf usually took the form of a big black wolf with long claws and green eyes. But when she was hungry she would close her eyes, smack her mouth, and turn into the prettiest woman you ever laid eyes on.

I reckon I got to interrupt the story right here to tell some of you boys who ain't got sense enough to keep your toenails cut short not to go around thinking that every pretty girl might be a witch. That ain't what the story say. The story is about *this* woman and her alone.

The Witch-Wolf's favorite activity was eating men. But before she ate them she would change into a pretty woman, make the man fall in love with her, and marry him. The "I do's" wouldn't be cold before she would shut her eyes, smack her mouth together, and change back into a wolf. Then she'd eat the man up, and that would be that.

One day word got back to her in the swamp that a new man had moved to town. He had land, but she didn't want the land. He had horses, but she didn't want the horses. He had cows, but she didn't want the cows. She wanted the man.

She closed her eyes, smacked her lips, and there she was, as pretty as a sunrise on a spring morning. Off she went.

The man was sitting on his porch in the cool of the day when a woman walked by, looking as good as a lawn that stays green and never has to be mowed.

"Evening," she said, real sweetlike.

"Good evening to you," he responded, sweating and trembling and grinning all at the same time.

"Mighty nice out this evening, ain't it?"

"It is that."

But before the man could say anything else, the woman walked on down the road, leaving him so eager to see her the next evening that he scarcely slept that night.

Every evening he sat on the porch and waited for her, and every evening she came by. Before long they were sitting on the porch drinking iced tea and talking about the kinds of things men and woman talk about.

The woman pretended that she was in love with him. He wasn't pretending about anything. He was sho' 'nuf in love, but something was holding him back. He wanted to ask her to marry him, but the words wouldn't come out of his mouth.

The man was in love but he wasn't dumb. Something about the woman didn't feel right. For one, where did she come from? She wouldn't tell him. Where did she live? She wouldn't tell him. Who were her people? How did she make a living? She wouldn't tell him.

But he decided to do some asking around. But who should he ask?

He studied on the situation for a while and finally decided to go see Judge Rabbit. He'd been living in them parts longer than anybody else.

The man went to Judge Rabbit's house and knocked on the door.

"Who's that?" Judge Rabbit called out.

"It's me," answered the man.

"Mighty short name for a grown man," Judge Rabbit said. "Give me the full entitlements."

The man gave out his full name, and Judge Rabbit let him in. They sat down by the fire, and the man started telling Judge Rabbit about the beautiful woman he had met.

"What's her name?" Judge Rabbit asked.

"Mizzle-Mazzle."

Judge Rabbit got very quiet. He made a mark in the ashes in the fireplace. "How old is she?"

The man told him.

Judge Rabbit made another mark. "Has she got eyes like a cat?"

The man thought for a moment. "I guess she does."

Judge Rabbit made another mark in the ashes. "Are her ears kind of pointed at the top?"

The man did more thinking. "They might be."

Judge Rabbit made yet another mark in the ashes. "Is her hair yellow?"

The man didn't need to worry his mind over that one. "Yes, it is."

Judge Rabbit made still another mark and frowned. "I thought Mizzle-Mazzle had moved out of the country. But here she is, galloping around, just as natural as a dead pig in the sunshine."

"What're you talking about, Judge?"

"If you want trouble with trouble that doubles and triples trouble, marry Mizzle-Mazzle."

The man looked scared. "What should I do?"

"You got any cows?"

"Plenty."

"Well, here's what you do. Ask Mizzle-Mazzle if she is a good housekeeper. She'll say yes. Ask her if she can cook. She'll say yes to that. Ask her if she can clean pots and pans. She'll say yes. Ask her if she can do the laundry. She'll say yes. Then ask her if she can milk the red cow. And watch what she says."

The man thanked Judge Rabbit and went home. When he got there, the woman was waiting for him.

"How you doing today?" he asked her.

"Fine. How you?"

"I ain't feeling too good," the man said.

"How come?"

"I'm not rightly sure. It might be because I'm lonely."

"Why are you lonely?"

"I guess it's because I ain't married."

The woman started batting her eyes real fast and running her tongue over her lipstick to make it shine. "What you looking for in a wife?"

"Well, I need somebody who can take care of the house when I'm gone and somebody to keep me company when I'm home. Are you a good housekeeper?"

"Why, yes. I am."

"Can you cook?"

"Why, yes."

"Can you clean pots and pans?"

"Indeed."

"Can you do the laundry?"

"Yes."

"Can you milk the red cow?"

The woman jumped and screamed so loud, the man almost fell over. "You don't think I'd let some cow kick me, do you?"

"The cow is as gentle as a baby."

The woman was still upset, but after a moment she said, "Well, I suppose I could try to milk the cow, if that's what you wanted me to do. But first, let me show you how well I can take care of a house."

Bright and early the next morning the woman came and cleaned the house from attic to cellar and back again.

The day after that she fixed him the best meal he had ever had. The day after that she cleaned the pots and pans. They shone so much like mirrors that Mr. Sun stayed a little longer at the man's house to look at himself in them.

The day after that she did the laundry and got the whites whiter than white, and the colored clothes stood up and started singing a commercial.

The day following that one, she came to milk the red cow. The man watched from a distance.

She walked into the cow pen with a pail. The cow smelled the witch in her blood. Cow snorted, pawed the ground, and lowered its head like it was going to charge. Before the woman knew it, that's just what the cow did.

The woman leaped the fence, and as she did so, smacked her lips together. She changed into a wolf and disappeared. She hasn't been seen from that time to this.

The Lottery

by Shirley Jackson

An acclaimed story first published in 1948 captures the sense of doom that pervades a peculiar small town at the beginning of summer. People have had strong reactions to "The Lottery" since it appeared. They have argued about what it means. Many critics believe the author was responding to World War II, which had recently ended. In addition, many people worried that communities were sometimes hostile to outsiders or to anyone who seemed different.

The morning of June 27th was clear and sunny, with the fresh warmth of a full-summer day; the flowers were blossoming profusely and the grass was richly green. The people of the village began to gather in the square, between the post office and the bank, around ten o'clock; in some towns there were so many people that the lottery took two days and had to be started on June 26th, but in this village, where there were only about three hundred people, the whole lottery took less than two hours, so it could begin at ten o'clock in the morning and still be through in time to allow the villagers to get home for noon dinner.

The children assembled first, of course. School was recently over for the summer, and the feeling of liberty sat uneasily on most of them; they tended to gather together quietly for a while before they broke into boisterous play, and their talk was still of the classroom and the teacher, of books and reprimands. Bobby Martin had already stuffed his pockets full of stones, and the other boys soon followed his example, selecting the smoothest and roundest stones; Bobby and Harry Jones and Dickie Delacroix—the villagers pronounced this name "Della-croy"—eventually made a great pile of stones in one corner of the square and guarded it against the raids of the other boys. The girls stood aside, talking among themselves, looking over their shoulders at the boys, and the very small children rolled in the dust or clung to the hands of their older brothers or sisters.

Soon the men began to gather, surveying their own children, speaking of planting and rain, tractors, and taxes. They stood together, away from the pile of stones in the corner, and their jokes were quiet and they smiled rather than laughed. The women, wearing faded house dresses and sweaters, came shortly after their menfolk. They greeted one another and exchanged bits of gossip as they went to join their husbands. Soon the women, standing by their husbands, began to call to their children, and the children came reluctantly, having to be called four or five times. Bobby Martin ducked under his mother's grasping hand and ran, laughing, back to the pile of stones. His father spoke up sharply, and Bobby came quickly and took his place between his father and his oldest brother.

The lottery was conducted—as were the square dances, the teen-age club, the Halloween program—by Mr. Summers, who had time and energy to devote to civic activities. He was a round-faced, jovial man and he ran the coal business, and people were sorry for him, because he had no children and his wife was a scold. When he arrived in the square, carrying the black wooden box, there was a murmur of conversation among the villagers, and he waved and called, "Little late today, folks." The postmaster, Mr. Graves, followed him, carrying a three-legged stool, and the stool was put in the center of the square and Mr. Summers set the black box down on it. The villagers kept their distance, leaving a space between themselves and the stool, and when Mr. Summers said, "Some of you fellows want to give me a hand?" there was a hesitation before two men, Mr. Martin and his oldest son, Baxter, came forward to hold the box steady on the stool while Mr. Summers stirred up the papers inside it.

The original paraphernalia for the lottery had been lost long ago, and the black box now resting on the stool had been put into use even before Old Man Warner, the oldest man in town, was born. Mr. Summers spoke frequently to the villagers about making a new box, but no one liked to upset even as much tradition as was represented by the black box. There was a story that the present box had been made with some pieces of the box that had preceded it, the one that had been constructed when the first people settled down to make a village here. Every year, after the lottery, Mr. Summers began talking again about a new box, but every year the subject was allowed to fade off without anything being done. The black box grew shabbier each year; by now it was no longer completely black but splintered badly along one side to show the original wood color, and in some places faded or stained.

Mr. Martin and his oldest son, Baxter, held the black box securely on the stool until Mr. Summers had stirred the papers thoroughly with his hand. Because so much of the ritual had been forgotten or discarded, Mr. Summers had been successful in having slips of paper substituted for the chips of wood that had been used for generations. Chips of wood, Mr. Summers had argued, had been all very well when the village was tiny, but now the population was more than three hundred and likely to keep on growing, it was necessary to use something that would fit more easily into the black box. The night before the lottery, Mr. Summers and Mr. Graves made up the slips of paper and put them in the box, and it was then taken to the safe of Mr. Summers' coal company and locked up until Mr. Summers was ready to take it to the square next morning. The rest of the year, the box was put away, sometimes one place, sometimes another; it had spent one year in Mr. Graves's barn and another year underfoot in the post office, and sometimes it was set on a shelf in the Martin grocery and left there.

There was a great deal of fussing to be done before Mr. Summers declared the lottery open. There were the lists to make up—of heads of families, heads of households in each family, members of each household in each family. There was the proper swearing-in of Mr. Summers by the postmaster, as the official of the lottery; at one time, some people remembered, there had been a recital of some sort, performed by the official of the lottery, a perfunctory, tuneless chant that had been rattled off duly each year; some people believed that the official of the lottery used to stand just so when he said or sang it, others believed that he was supposed to walk among the people, but years and years ago this part of the ritual had been allowed to lapse. There had been, also, a ritual salute, which the official of the lottery had had to use in addressing each person who came up to draw from the box, but this also had changed with time, until now it was felt necessary only for the official to speak to each person approaching. Mr. Summers was very good at all this; in his clean white shirt and blue jeans, with one hand resting carelessly on the black box, he seemed very proper and important as he talked interminably to Mr. Graves and the Martins.

Just as Mr. Summers finally left off talking and turned to the assembled villagers, Mrs. Hutchinson came hurriedly along the path to the square, her sweater thrown over her shoulders, and slid into place in the back of the crowd. "Clean forgot what day it was," she said to Mrs. Delacroix, who stood next to her, and they both laughed softly. "Thought my old man was out back stacking wood," Mrs. Hutchinson went on, "and then I looked out the window and the kids was gone, and then I remembered it was the twenty-seventh and came a-running." She dried her hands on her apron, and Mrs. Delacroix said, "You're in time, though. They're still talking away up there."

Mrs. Hutchinson craned her neck to see through the crowd and found her husband and children standing near the front. She tapped Mrs. Delacroix on the arm as a farewell and began to make her way through the crowd. The people separated good-humoredly to let her through; two or three people said, in voices just loud enough to be heard across the crowd, "Here comes your Missus, Hutchinson," and "Bill, she made it after all." Mrs. Hutchinson reached her husband, and Mr. Summers, who had been waiting, said cheerfully, "Thought we were going to have to get on without you, Tessie." Mrs. Hutchinson said, grinning, "Wouldn't have me leave m'dishes in the sink, now, would you, Joe?" and soft laughter ran through the crowd as the people stirred back into position after Mrs. Hutchinson's arrival.

"Well, now," Mr. Summers said soberly, "guess we better get started, get this over with, so's we can go back to work. Anybody ain't here?"

"Dunbar," several people said. "Dunbar, Dunbar."

Mr. Summers consulted his list. "Clyde Dunbar," he said. "That's right. He's broke his leg, hasn't he? Who's drawing for him?"

"Me, I guess," a woman said, and Mr. Summers turned to look at her. "Wife draws for her husband," Mr. Summers said. "Don't you have a

96

grown boy to do it for you, Janey?" Although Mr. Summers and every-one else in the village knew the answer perfectly well, it was the business of the official of the lottery to ask such questions formally. Mr. Summers waited with an expression of polite interest while Mrs. Dunbar answered.

"Horace's not but 16 yet," Mrs. Dunbar said regretfully. "Guess I gotta fill in for the old man this year."

"Right," Mr. Summers said. He made a note on the list he was holding. Then he asked, "Watson boy drawing this year?"

A tall boy in the crowd raised his hand. "Here," he said. "I'm drawing for m'mother and me." He blinked his eyes nervously and ducked his head as several voices in the crowd said things like "Good fellow, Jack," and "Glad to see your mother's got a man to do it."

"Well," Mr. Summers said, "guess that's everyone. Old Man Warner make it?"

"Here," a voice said, and Mr. Summers nodded.

A sudden hush fell on the crowd as Mr. Summers cleared his throat and looked at the list. "All ready?" he called. "Now, I'll read the names—heads of the families first—and the men come up and take a paper out of the box. Keep the paper folded in your hand without looking at it until everyone has had a turn. Everything clear?"

The people had done it so many times that they only half listened to the directions; most of them were quiet, wetting their lips, not looking around. Then Mr. Summers raised one hand high and said, "Adams." A man disengaged himself from the crowd and came forward. "Hi, Steve," Mr. Summers said, and Mr. Adams said, "Hi, Joe." They grinned at one another humorlessly and nervously. Then Mr. Adams reached into the black box and took out a folded paper. He held it firmly by one corner as he turned and went hastily back to his place in the crowd, where he stood a little apart from his family, not looking down at his hand.

"Allen," Mr. Summers said. "Anderson. . . . Benthan."

"Seems like there's no time at all between lotteries any more," Mrs. Delacroix said to Mrs. Graves in the back row. "Seems like we got through with the last one only last week."

"Time sure goes fast," Mrs. Graves said.

"Clark. . . . Delacroix."

"There goes my old man," Mrs. Delacroix said. She held her breath while her husband went forward.

"Dunbar," Mr. Summers said, and Mrs. Dunbar went steadily to the box while one of the women said, "Go on, Janey," and another said, "There she goes."

"We're next," Mrs. Graves said. She watched while Mr. Graves came around from the side of the box, greeted Mr. Summers gravely, and selected a slip of paper from the box. By now, all through the crowd there were men holding the small folded papers in their large hands, turning them over and over nervously. Mrs. Dunbar and her two sons stood together, Mrs. Dunbar holding the slip of paper.

"Harburt. . . . Hutchinson."

"Get up there, Bill," Mrs. Hutchinson said, and the people near her laughed.

"Jones."

"They do say," Mr. Adams said to Old Man Warner, who stood next to him, "that over in the north village they're talking of giving up the lottery."

Old Man Warner snorted. "Pack of crazy fools," he said. "Listening to the young folks, nothing's good enough for *them*. Next thing you know, they'll be wanting to go back to living in caves, nobody work any more, live *that* way for a while. Used to be a saying about 'Lottery in June, corn be heavy soon.' First thing you know, we'd all be eating chickweed and acorns. There's *always* been a lottery," he added petulantly. "Bad enough to see young Joe Summers up there joking with everybody."

"Some places have already quit lotteries," Mrs. Adams said.

"Nothing but trouble in *that*," Old Man Warner said stoutly. "Pack of young fools."

"Martin." And Bobby Martin watched his father go forward. "Overdyke. . . . Percy."

"I wish they'd hurry," Mrs. Dunbar said to her older son. "I wish they'd hurry."

"They're almost through," her son said.

"You get ready to run tell Dad," Mrs. Dunbar said.

Mr. Summers called his own name and then stepped forward precisely and selected a slip from the box. Then he called, "Warner."

"Seventy-seventh year I been in the lottery," Old Man Warner said as he went through the crowd. "Seventy-seventh time."

"Watson." The tall boy came awkwardly through the crowd. Someone said, "Don't be nervous, Jack," and Mr. Summers said, "Take your time, son."

"Zanini."

After that, there was a long pause, a breathless pause, until Mr. Summers, holding his slip of paper in the air, said, "All right, fellows." For a minute, no one moved, and then all the slips of paper were opened. Suddenly, all the women began to speak at once, saying, "Who is it?," "Who's got it?," "Is it the Dunbars?," "Is it the Watsons?" Then the voices began to say, "It's Hutchinson. It's Bill," "Bill Hutchinson's got it."

"Go tell your father," Mrs. Dunbar said to her older son.

People began to look around to see the Hutchinsons. Bill Hutchinson was standing quiet, staring down at the paper in his hand. Suddenly, Tessie Hutchinson shouted to Mr. Summers, "You didn't give him time enough to take any paper he wanted. I saw you. It wasn't fair!"

"Be a good sport, Tessie," Mrs. Delacroix called, and Mrs. Graves said, "All of us took the same chance."

"Shut up, Tessie," Bill Hutchinson said.

"Well, everyone," Mr. Summers said, "that was done pretty fast, and now we've got to be hurrying a little more to get done in time." He consulted his next list. "Bill," he said, "you draw for the Hutchinson family. You got any other households in the Hutchinsons?"

"There's Don and Eva," Mrs. Hutchinson yelled. "Make them take their chance!"

"Daughters draw with their husbands' families, Tessie," Mr. Summers said gently. "You know that as well as anyone else."

"It wasn't *fair*," Tessie said.

"I guess not, Joe," Bill Hutchinson said regretfully. "My daughter draws with her husband's family, that's only fair. And I've got no other family except the kids."

"Then, as far as drawing for families is concerned, it's you," Mr. Summers said in explanation, "and as far as drawing for households is concerned, that's you, too. Right?"

"Right," Bill Hutchinson said.

"How many kids, Bill?" Mr. Summers asked formally.

"Three," Bill Hutchinson said. "There's Bill, Jr., and Nancy, and little Dave. And Tessie and me."

"All right, then," Mr. Summers said. "Harry, you got their tickets back?"

Mr. Graves nodded and held up the slips of paper. "Put them in the box, then," Mr. Summers directed. "Take Bill's and put it in."

"I think we ought to start over," Mrs. Hutchinson said, as quietly as she could. "I tell you it wasn't *fair.* You didn't give him time enough to choose. *Everybody* saw that."

Mr. Graves had selected the five slips and put them in the box, and he dropped all the papers but those onto the ground, where the breeze caught them and lifted them off.

"Listen, everybody," Mrs. Hutchinson was saying to the people around her.

"Ready, Bill?" Mr. Summers asked, and Bill Hutchinson, with one quick glance around at his wife and children, nodded.

"Remember," Mr. Summers said, "take the slips and keep them folded until each person has taken one. Harry, you help little Dave." Mr. Graves took the hand of the little boy, who came willingly with him up to the box. "Take a paper out of the box, Davy," Mr. Summers said. Davy put his hand into the box and laughed. "Take just *one* paper," Mr. Summers said. "Harry, you hold it for him." Mr. Graves took the child's hand and removed the folded paper from the tight fist and held it while little Dave stood next to him and looked up at him wonderingly.

"Nancy next," Mr. Summers said. Nancy was twelve, and her school friends breathed heavily as she went forward, switching her skirt, and took a slip daintily from the box. "Bill, Jr.," Mr. Summers said, and Billy, his face red and his feet over-large, nearly knocked the box over as he got a paper out. "Tessie," Mr. Summers said. She hesitated for a minute, looking around defiantly, and then set her lips and went up to the box. She snatched a paper out and held it behind her.

"Bill," Mr. Summers said, and Bill Hutchinson reached into the box and felt around, bringing his hand out at last with the slip of paper in it.

The crowd was quiet. A girl whispered, "I hope it's not Nancy," and the sound of the whisper reached the edges of the crowd.

"It's not the way it used to be," Old Man Warner said clearly. "People ain't the way they used to be."

"All right," Mr. Summers said. "Open the papers. Harry, you open little Dave's."

Mr. Graves opened the slip of paper and there was a general sigh through the crowd as he held it up and everyone could see it was blank. Nancy and Bill, Jr., opened theirs at the same time, and both beamed and laughed, turning around to the crowd and holding their slips of paper above their heads.

"Tessie," Mr. Summers said. There was a pause, and then Mr. Summers looked at Bill Hutchinson, and Bill unfolded his paper and showed it. It was blank.

"It's Tessie," Mr. Summers said, and his voice was hushed. "Show us her paper, Bill."

Bill Hutchinson went over to his wife and forced the slip of paper out of her hand. It had a black spot on it, the black spot Mr. Summers had made the night before with the heavy pencil in the coal-company office. Bill Hutchinson held it up, and there was a stir in the crowd.

"All right, folks," Mr. Summers said. "Let's finish quickly."

Although the villagers had forgotten the ritual and lost the original black box, they still remembered to use stones. The pile of stones the boys had made earlier was ready; there were stones on the ground with the blowing scraps of paper that had come out of the box. Mrs. Delacroix selected a stone so large she had to pick it up with both hands and turned to Mrs. Dunbar. "Come on," she said. "Hurry up."

Mrs. Dunbar had small stones in both hands, and she said, gasping for breath, "I can't run at all. You'll have to go ahead and I'll catch up with you."

The children had stones already, and someone gave little Davy Hutchinson a few pebbles.

Tessie Hutchinson was in the center of a cleared space by now, and she held her hands out desperately as the villagers moved in on her. "It isn't fair," she said. A stone hit her on the side of the head.

Old Man Warner was saying, "Come on, come on, everyone." Steve Adams was in the front of the crowd of villagers, with Mrs. Graves beside him.

"It isn't fair, it isn't right," Mrs. Hutchinson screamed, and then they were upon her.

The Secret

by Ilana Girard Singer

A mood of deep fear and suspicion swept the United States during the 1950s. Many Americans became convinced that hidden Communists were plotting the overthrow of the government. Teachers, writers, and government workers accused of being Communists or Communist sympathizers lost their jobs. This memoir depicts the impact of that time, when neighbors viewed one another with mistrust.

I loved going to my neighbor Patti's house. She had a TV and we didn't. Sometimes, we'd sit with her mother on their turquoise couch beneath a picture of pink flamingos and sing along with *Your Hit Parade.* Her mother looked just like Doris Day and wore red nail polish. Sometimes she played jacks with Patti and me.

One morning I knocked on Patti's door, but this time her mother didn't greet me with a smile. Patti wasn't home, she said. Her voice was cold. "Aren't your parents foreign-born?" she asked. "What nationality are you?"

"I'm American," I said warily. My parents had warned me about hidden loyalty questions. Patti's mother asked me outright, "Is your father a Communist?" I felt as though I'd been stabbed. I stammered, "No. He's a Progressive," and ran back home, confused and afraid I'd given away "The Secret."

"The Secret" made me feel different and scared. Each morning at my elementary school in the San Francisco suburbs, I said the Pledge of Allegiance, just like other kids. But in 1954, when I was in the fifth grade, the Pledge changed. Now when I placed my hand over my heart, I recited the Pledge but, as my parents had instructed me, I refused to say, "under God," which had been inserted in the phrase, "one nation indivisible." Father explained that in America, unlike the Tsar's Russia where he was born, our Constitution separates church and state.

I tried to fit in, but the bullies pointed at my pink glasses and called me "egghead" and "four eyes." They snickered at my mismatched skirts and blouses, which my mother had bought at the rummage sale for the *People's World*, a Communist newspaper. Sometimes they pulled my braids until I cried.

They laughed and made fun of me because I didn't know who Buffalo Bob and Clarabelle the Clown were. They couldn't believe I'd never seen the *Howdy Doody Show*. How could I have? Father called TV a propaganda machine.

Then there were the bomb drills. Our teacher told us the windows were reinforced with chicken wire to protect us from flying glass when the Russian bombs exploded. One day, the sirens whined and Miss Meadows barked: "Drop! . . . Cover up and shut your eyes!" I scrunched underneath my desk, my legs cramping, my back to the windows, just like the other kids.

"Who drops these bombs?" one boy called out.

"The Jews. The Reds. The Commies!" another answered. I looked around. Who were they accusing? Did they know about my father the Russian, the Communist, the Jew?

Father was headmaster at San Francisco's Die Kindershule (The Children's School). Each Sunday I studied there with my true friends—children like me from secular, labor, and Communist families. I attended Father's Jewish history class. His dark eyes were intent behind his wire-rimmed spectacles as he told stories about how Jews were an oppressed people—enslaved by the Pharaohs, burned at the stake during the Spanish Inquisition, and exterminated by the Nazis. At Die Kindershule, no religion was taught, no Hebrew prayers and no Torah. We did not celebrate Yom Kippur or Rosh

Hashanah, or even hear the ram's horn. Instead, we celebrated holidays of political freedom and emancipation such as Purim, Chanukah, Passover. I loved seder. I loved decorating the long tables with white bedsheets and spring blossoms for our seventy Kindershule families who celebrated together. In 1954 my father wrote a special Haggadah emphasizing dignity and emancipation. On each student's mimeographed copy he wrote a little note. I still have mine, his inscription hand-printed in the corner: "Sweet Ilana, many happy Pesachs to you, daddy Al."

The story of Pesach—escaping oppression—was my father's story. He'd fled persecution in Siberia to Harbin, China, where he grew up along with hundreds of Russian Jews. When he was a teen, he immigrated to Seattle, Washington, to study at the university. Later he became a political activist in California, organizing migrant workers and leading protests against unsafe working conditions and high food prices. Father was charismatic. He stood on soap boxes and spoke to street-corner crowds, demanding unemployment insurance and Social Security for all Americans.

Father was also a charismatic teacher. The Die Kindershule children loved the stories he told about struggling peoples—Jews, Irish, Mexican. He made American Negro heroes come alive for us: Harriet Tubman, Nat Turner, and the Scottsboro Boys. Like us, they were former slaves.

Paul Robeson was the son of a former slave, a black activist, actor, and opera singer. He was barred from concert halls all over the country because he was a Communist. So my parents and their friends organized Robeson's concert in an Oakland ghetto church. That evening, as he sang to an overflowing crowd of Jews, Christians, Negroes, whites, Latinos, Asians, longshoremen, teachers, lawyers, I handed him roses. I wore my hair in my Russian-style braids. I was so proud.

Pete Seeger, another blacklisted singer, brought his banjo to Die Kindershule, where we sang folk songs at a hootenanny. I loved the one about striking miners fighting the capitalist owners. I bellowed its refrain: "Which side are you on? Which side are you on?" I was always choosing sides, always trying to fit in.

Father must have understood my conflict because he encouraged me to think for myself. My schoolbooks were boring, so he gave me books about real people, about suffering and injustice: stories of the children in the Warsaw ghetto, Howard Fast's *Sacco and Vanzetti*, about the Italian anarchists who were executed, Michael Gold's *Jews Without Money*, about poor immigrant Jews in New York.

It was not safe to keep certain books at home during the McCarthy era. Many Americans were suspicious of anyone who read "too much." That's why my parents told me never to let neighbors into our house. They'd see our house was crammed full of "subversive" magazines, newspapers, and books that had been banned and removed from library shelves in many states. They might snitch to the FBI that we had many of these banned volumes, books by Thomas Paine, Emile Zola, Upton Sinclair, and Dante. Even my beloved book *Robin Hood* had been called "Communist doctrine." I had to be careful.

Father taught me how to spot the FBI men in snap-brimmed fedoras and gray flannel suits. They looked like "Fuller Brush" salesmen, but without the sample cases. One day Mother was in the backyard hanging out the wash and Father, an electrical engineer, was at work. I answered the doorbell and saw two stiff-looking men who asked to see my mother. I knew who they were and just as my parents had taught me, I tried to shut the door, but one of them stuck out his foot and blocked my attempt.

Mother came in and saw me struggling. She nudged me aside, but I hid behind our bookcases, listening, as they interrogated her. "Give us names of your friends and we'll help you," said one of the men. "We know you're not a citizen."

Her voice trembled as she told them to go away. Although Mother, a Canadian citizen, was a permanent resident and a legal alien, she was afraid of deportation. After the FBI men drove away, she left me alone in the house and rushed out to a pay phone to call her attorney. We didn't use our own telephone because it was tapped.

One night after a hootenany at Die Kindershule, my father was driving us home and telling my little brother and me the story of Robin Hood. Suddenly, he stopped the story.

"I'll pull over and park," he said abruptly. "I'll tell them I know they're FBI." But Mother urged him to keep driving, to lose them in the hills. Father zigzagged through the dark, narrow roads, trying to shake free from those headlights behind us that kept piercing the veil of fog. "The FBI wants us to know they're following us," my father explained. The FBI was trying to intimidate us and I was scared.

Even when my family listened to the radio, I was afraid. On June 19, 1953, we were listening to Berkeley's KPFA, America's first member-sponsored, public broadcasting radio station. It was accused of being run by "subversives."

We heard the announcer say that Julius and Ethel Rosenberg, the Jewish couple convicted of selling atomic secrets to the Soviet Union, had just been executed. I imagined I was one of the two Rosenberg sons, Robby and Michael, in the death chamber of Sing Sing Prison trying to unstrap my parents from the electric chair. But it was too late ... too late ...

I was very sad for their sons, and lived in fear that if I gave away our secret, my parents could get taken away.

The Peace of Wild Things

by Wendell Berry

When despair for the world grows in me
and I wake in the night at the least sound
in fear of what my life and my children's lives may be,
I go and lie down where the wood drake
rests in his beauty on the water, and the great heron feeds.
I come into the peace of wild things
who do not tax their lives with forethought
of grief. I come into the presence of still water.
And I feel above me the day-blind stars
waiting with their light. For a time
I rest in the grace of the world, and am free.

Democracy

by E.B. White

In addition to writing some of the best-loved children's books of all time, including Charlotte's Web, *E. B. White was an essayist reknowned for his clear, graceful style, as in this piece written during World War II.*

We received a letter from the Writers' War Board the other day asking for a statement on "The Meaning of Democracy." It presumably is our duty to comply with such a request, and it is certainly our pleasure.

Surely the Board knows what democracy is. It is the line that forms on the right. It is the don't in Don't Shove. It is the hole in the stuffed shirt through which the sawdust slowly trickles; it is the dent in the high hat. Democracy is the recurrent suspicion that more than half of the people are right more than half of the time. It is the feeling of privacy in the voting booths, the feeling of communion in the libraries, the feeling of vitality everywhere. Democracy is a letter to the editor. Democracy is the score at the beginning of the ninth. It is an idea that hasn't been disproved yet, a song the words of which have not gone bad. It's the mustard on the hot dog and the cream in the rationed coffee. Democracy is a request from a War Board, in the middle of a morning in the middle of a war, wanting to know what democracy is.

Tattoo

by Gregg Shapiro

My father won't talk about the numbers
3-7-8-2-5 between the wrist and elbow
blue as blood on his left forearm
Instead, he spreads himself over me
spilling his protection, like acid, until it burns
I wear him like a cloak, sweat under the weight

There were stories in the lines on his face
the nervous blue flash in his eyes
his bone-crushing hugs
I am drowning in his silence
trying to stay afloat on curiosity
Questions choke me and I swallow hard

We don't breathe the same air
speak the same language
live in the same universe
We are continents, worlds apart
I am sorry my life has remained unscathed
His scars still bleed, his bruises don't fade

If I could trade places with him
I would pad the rest of his days
wrap him in gauze and velvet
absorb the shocks and treat his wounds
I would scrub the numbers from his flesh
extinguish the fire and give him back his life

Visas for Life

by David Tracey

Non-Jews who helped save Jews during the Holocaust have been called "righteous gentiles," and many of them have been honored for their bravery. Priests, nuns, diplomats, businessmen, and ordinary people sheltered or aided Jews who were trying to escape the Nazis. Thousands more people would have been killed if it were not for these strangers who took it upon themselves to help. The following is a true account of one of these people.

Sempo Sugihara awoke to shouts outside the Japanese consulate in Kaunas, Lithuania. Through a window, the 40-year-old diplomat stared in disbelief at hundreds of men, women and children.

Many of the men were bearded and wore long black caftans and round fur hats. Some of the people held babies or supported grandparents. Most carried all they owned in cloth-wrapped bundles.

"They're Jewish refugees," a houseboy informed Sugihara. "They want you to save their lives."

It was July 27, 1940. The previous September, Germany had invaded Poland, and horrifying reports of German crimes against Jews were spreading. But what could that have to do with a minor Japanese diplomat in Lithuania? Sugihara asked for a meeting, and Zorach Warhaftig, a lawyer in his mid-30s, explained the plight of his people.

Entire families were being slaughtered by the Nazis, Warhaftig told

Sugihara. The refugees had managed to reach Russian-dominated Lithuania, but it was only a matter of time before the war came here as well.

Only one escape route remained—overland through the Soviet Union. But the Russians would never let them pass without proof that the Jews would be admitted to another country after crossing the Soviet Union. Other consulates in Lithuania were either unsympathetic or closed.

Thousands of visas would be needed. "I want to help you," Sugihara said, "but I will have to ask Tokyo."

Warhaftig worried. Few countries in 1940 were willing to help homeless Jews, and Japan was about to be formally allied with Germany.

Standing in the crowd that day was Yehoshua Nishri, 20. He listened as Warhaftig gave them a report. This is our only hope, he thought. Time is running out.

Sugihara cabled the foreign ministry in Tokyo, explaining the plight of the Jews. "I am requesting permission to issue transit visas immediately," he wrote.

Two days later the response arrived. With dismay, Sugihara read: "You are not to issue transit visas to those people who do not have a designated destination."

That night Sugihara paced the floor until dawn. "I must do something," he told his wife, Yukiko, who had stayed up with him.

"Yes," Yukiko said. "We have to." She thought sadly of the "No Jews Allowed" sign at the public park. *How could people turn their hearts over to blind hate?* she wondered. The look of desperation in the eyes of the refugees—especially those with small children—had moved the young mother of three sons.

Sugihara cabled Tokyo again, explaining that the refugees would need 20 days to cross the Soviet Union. Following the boat trip from the Russian port of Vladivostok, they would have 30 days in Japan. Surely in 50 days, he argued, a final destination could be found.

The answer was still no.

Sugihara sent a third cable to Tokyo explaining that with a Nazi advance imminent, the Jews had nowhere else to turn. Again, his request was denied. The choice for Sempo Sugihara was clear: he would have to obey either his government or his conscience.

Sempo Sugihara always went his own way. He graduated from high school with top marks, and his father insisted that he become a doctor. But Sempo's dream was to study literature and live abroad.

On the morning of the entrance exam for premedical students, young Sugihara left home with his father's admonition to do his best. But when the exams were handed out, he wrote his name on the top and then set his pencil down. When the test was over, he turned in a blank sheet.

Sugihara entered Tokyo's prestigious Waseda University to study English. He paid for his own education with part-time work as a longshoreman, tutor, and rickshaw-puller.

One day he saw an intriguing item in the want ads. The foreign ministry was seeking young people who wished to study abroad as a start to a diplomatic career. It seemed perfect for the young dreamer. One of only a handful to pass the demanding test, Sugihara was sent to university in Harbin, China. There he studied Russian. He also converted to Christianity.

After graduating with honors, he took a job with the Japanese-controlled government in Manchuria, in northeastern China. He rose to become vice minister of the foreign-affairs department. One time when the Soviet government offered to sell a railway to the Japanese, Sugihara researched the deal. After discovering that the Soviet price was double what the railway was worth, he got the price cut in half.

Such initiative soon put Sugihara one step away from becoming the minister of foreign affairs in Manchuria. But he became dismayed at the cruel way his countrymen were treating the local people. Sugihara resigned as vice minister in protest and returned to Japan in 1934.

Since he was now the top Russian-speaker in the Japanese government, the foreign ministry hoped to post him to the Moscow embassy. But the Soviets remembered the railway deal and refused to allow Sugihara in. Tokyo sent him instead to Lithuania to open a one-man consulate in 1939. There he could report on Soviet activities and German war plans.

Six months later, war erupted and the Soviet Union annexed Lithuania. All the consulates were to be closed. And the crowd of Jews outside Sugihara's gate was growing by the hour.

Sugihara and his wife discussed what might happen if he disobeyed orders. "It could mean the end of my career," he said. But in the end, Sugihara knew which path he would follow.

"I may have to disobey the government," he told Yukiko. "But if I don't, I would be disobeying God."

Outside the consulate, Sugihara announced to the crowd, "I will issue a transit visa to everyone who wants one."

There was shocked silence, then an explosion of joy. Many wept in prayer. A long, disorderly line formed as people jostled for position.

Since the Japanese visas were for transit only, the holder would still need to declare a final destination. Curaçao, a Dutch possession in the Caribbean, was suggested. Warhaftig had obtained a written statement saying no visa was required to enter the colony.

Sugihara began issuing visas that morning of August 1. At first he asked all applicants the standard questions: Did they have travel tickets to take them beyond Japan? Did they have enough money for the trip? But when it became obvious that many of the refugees had fled with few possessions, Sugihara omitted these questions.

Igo Feldblum, 12, and his family had escaped from Krakow, Poland. When it was their turn to enter Sugihara's office, one of the consul's assistants whispered a phrase to each member of Igo's family: *Banzai Nippon* (Long live Japan). With these words, Sugihara could confirm that the refugees "spoke Japanese."

Each visa took about a quarter of an hour. Sugihara skipped lunch to write as many as possible. Even so, when he finally stopped that first night, the crowds had not diminished.

He worked day and night, and when the official forms ran out, he wrote more by hand. As the days went by, Sugihara began to weaken. His eyes become bloodshot from lack of sleep. "I wonder if I should stop now," he wearily told his wife one night.

"Let's save as many as we can," Yukiko softly answered.

By the third week of August, Sugihara had received cables ordering him to stop. Large numbers of Polish refugees were arriving in the Japanese ports of Yokohama and Kobe, creating chaos. Sugihara ignored the orders.

By the end of August, the Soviets were demanding that the consulate be shut down. Tokyo instructed Sugihara to move to Berlin. Yet hundreds of Jews were still arriving. The pleading faces in the crowd were too much to bear. "We will be staying for one night at a hotel here," Sugihara announced. "I will issue as many visas as I can before we leave."

A crowd followed the family to the hotel, where Sugihara continued to write. The next morning, an even larger group followed Sugihara and his family to the train station. On the train, he continued to scribble frantically, but he couldn't produce enough visas for everyone. He began signing his name on blank sheets of paper, hoping that the rest might be filled in. He was still passing papers through the window as the train pulled away.

"Sempo Sugihara," a man shouted down the tracks, "we will never forget you!"

Clutching their precious visas, the refugees made their way east across Siberia. By the time they found themselves safely aboard a ship bound for Japan, many Jews were convinced that Sugihara's hastily penned and stamped pieces of paper had somehow been blessed.

Moshe Cohen, a 17-year-old seminary student, certainly thought so. As his group started to board the ship for Kobe, Cohen watched a Russian official shove a rabbi toward two Japanese officials checking visas. When the rabbi opened his passport, the wind blew away his visa, carrying it out in a fluttering arc over the water.

"We all watched, transfixed," says Cohen. "Around it flew until it landed back on the ramp, right at the rabbi's feet. He handed it to the Japanese officials, who waved him through."

In Japan, the Jews were treated without discrimination. When their transit visas expired, they were allowed to go to Shanghai to wait out the war. Curaçao, it turned out, was closed to them. After the war some settled in Japan. Most of the others traveled to the United States, South America, or Palestine, the future state of Israel.

Sugihara estimated that he wrote 3,500 transit visas. Other sources say at least 6,000.

During the war, Sugihara headed consulates in Czechoslovakia, Romania, and Germany. Since the visas were never mentioned by his government, he thought his actions had been forgotten.

In 1945 Sugihara was running the Japanese consulate in Bucharest, Romania, when he and his family were arrested by Soviet troops and taken to a prison camp. After 21 months, the family was returned to Japan.

Back in Tokyo, Sugihara was hoping to be offered an ambassadorship. Instead, the vice foreign minister asked for his resignation. The customary letter of recommendation was denied. Sugihara realized that they had remembered what he had done in Lithuania.

To support his family, the career diplomat first tried selling lightbulbs door-to-door. Eventually he moved to Moscow to manage a branch of a trading firm, leaving his family behind for long periods of time.

The Jews whose lives he saved never forgot Sugihara. Many tried to find him; their inquiries to the foreign ministry in Tokyo were fruitless.

One day in 1967, Sugihara's son Hiroki received a message that an official at the Israeli embassy in Tokyo wanted to see him. It was Yehoshua Nishri, who had the family tracked through the Japanese foreign ministry alumni list.

"I've been looking for your father for years," Nishri told Hiroki. "I could never forget the man who saved my life."

Hiroki said that his father was working in Moscow. "Tell him that Israel wants to honor him for what he did," Nishri said.

Hiroki received a typical answer from his father: he was busy with his job and had no time for official thanks. But three months later, Nishri convinced Sugihara to come to Israel.

In Tel Aviv, Sugihara was greeted as a hero. Parties were held in his honor by the people he had saved, some of whom had gone on to play important roles in Israel's young history. Among them was Zorach Warhaftig, who had helped write Israel's declaration of independence and was now minister of religious affairs.

"I've always wondered," Warhaftig said, "why you did it."

Sugihara replied, "I saw people in distress, and I was able to help them, so why shouldn't I?"

In 1984 Israel's Holocaust Martyrs' and Heroes' Remembrance Authority awarded Sugihara the title of "Righteous Among the Nations." Sugihara, 85, was too frail to attend the ceremony, so his wife accepted the award. A park was named after him, and in 1992, Israel awarded Sugihara a commemorative citizenship.

Sugihara has been honored in the United States too. Recently the Mirrer Yeshiva, a religious school, celebrated its 50th anniversary in New York City. The school's entire faculty and student body—some 300 rabbis, students, and family members—fled Mir, Poland, and were saved by Sugihara. The anniversary was celebrated with the establishment of the Sempo Sugihara Educational Fund to benefit young Jewish scholars.

Igo Feldblum is now a physician living in Haifa, Israel. "A brave man does things which are difficult to do," he reflects. "A hero does things which seem impossible to do. He acted even though he knew he would gain nothing from it."

Sugihara died in Japan in relative obscurity in 1986. Only when a large number of Orthodox Jews showed up at his home for the funeral service did his neighbors even realize they'd been living next door to a hero.

In 1991, the Japanese government issued a belated apology to his family for firing him. His wife and sons still hear from thankful Jews who received one of Sugihara's visas. It is estimated that if the children and grandchildren of the people he saved are counted, there are tens of thousands around the world who owe their lives to the courageous diplomat.

Warhaftig, who has 25 grandchildren, looks back on the experience and says, "Sempo Sugihara was an emissary of God."

The Narrow Man

by Anne Howard Bailey

Prejudice can present itself as something noble, as in this television play written in the 1950s. A wealthy businessman offers to endow a struggling college, but his gift has certain conditions. Are the requirements too disturbing for the college president to accept, or are they a reasonable way to serve the community?

CHARACTERS

ALEX THORNTON, *dynamic young president of Bradford College. He's in his late 30s.*

SUSAN THORNTON, *Alex's wife. Charming and gracious. In her middle 30s.*

PROFESSOR ADAM WOOLSEY, *retiring Head of the History Department. Crotchety, eccentric and incorruptible. In his 60s.*

PAUL RUDOLPH, *a senior student, who is brilliant in science and weak in history. He wears a chip on his shoulder. He's in his 20s.*

BURTON BRYCE, *local millionaire. A bitter and prejudiced man in his mid-60s.*

ACT ONE

FADE IN: *Modest-sized college building. Film clip of Neo-Gothic architecture.* CUT TO: *CU of bronze plaque. It reads:*

BRADFORD COLLEGE
FOUNDED 1865

DISSOLVE TO: *Thornton living room. Pleasant and shabby. A late May afternoon. The sun slants in open casement windows.* PAUL RUDOLPH, *a lean, intense lad of 20, fidgets as he models a black graduation robe, much the worse for age and wear.* SUSAN THORNTON, *a slim, vivacious 35, kneels in front of him, pinning up the hem.*

SUSAN: Let's see you, Paul. [*Peers up*] Ummm . . . very scholarly. Even if you *are* all pins.

PAUL: I know. I'm afraid to breathe. Can I take if off now?

SUSAN: Yes. But be careful. These robes tear like paper, they're so old. [*Beat.*] Maybe next year we can see about getting new ones!

PAUL: Is there going to be a next year? [SUSAN *reacts. Looks at him sharply. He goes on hastily.*] You know how you hear things on the grapevine? They're saying the college has gone broke. It might not open next fall!

SUSAN [*hesitantly*]: I think . . . Dr. Thornton should talk to you about this. . . . [*Calls*] Alex!

ALEX [*from O.S.*]: Be right there, Susan! Have you seen my briefcase?

SUSAN [*project*]: It's on your desk. Where you put it.

    [ALEX THORNTON, *a handsome, distinguished man in late 30s, enters from hall.*]

ALEX [*grins, as he sees briefcase*]: The one place I didn't look!

SUSAN: Paul says the student body has been hearing rumors that Bradford might close.

PAUL: It would be rough on the undergrads! Lot of kids can't afford to finish out in another school. They can't swing the tuition. They're pretty worried.

ALEX: I'm pretty worried myself, Paul. Because the thing that gives Bradford its value . . . our low tuition . . . is the thing that's driving us out of existence. We don't take in enough money to meet expenses—and we haven't any endowment to fall back on.

PAUL: Yeah, I see. If you raise the tuition—you shut out a bunch of students who need, and want, a college education.

ALEX: That's the problem. [*A grin*] How would you solve it?

PAUL [*grins back*]: Find a rich sucker!

ALEX: I've been looking for one for years! [*Pause . . . then gravely*]

When I first was made president here, I used to dream of snagging a big donation or endowment for the college. Oh—I built a new library...a new gym...new dormitories...all in my mind.Well, time passes, Paul...and even dreams get more realistic. I'd settle now for a few thousand dollars...to pay the taxes, and the light bill...and the faculty. The smallest possible amount of money...that would keep us open...! And even that's too much to hope for!

[*He turns abruptly. Starts for the door.* SUSAN *follows.*]

SUSAN: Alex, if it has to be—it has to be! You must reconcile yourself!

[ALEX *shakes his head. Then* ...]

ALEX: I'll be late for dinner.The Board of Trustees is meeting to make a decision. [*Heavily*] I'll have to recommend the college be closed.

SUSAN: Alex...listen! It isn't *your* failure! You've done your best!

ALEX: Well—it wasn't good enough.

[*He exits.* SUSAN *looks after him, troubled and distressed.*]

PAUL [*sympathetically*]: Dr.Thornton's taking it hard.

SUSAN: Yes.

PAUL [*glances at watch. Reacts.*]: Oh—oh...I'll be late for Woolsey.

SUSAN [*puzzled*]: History class—*this* time of day?

PAUL: Private session. I think he's gonna tell me he's flunking me!

SUSAN [*aghast*]: Paul!

PAUL: I'm not worried. I'll bone up a couple of nights before the exam—

SUSAN: Why don't you start cramming now?

PAUL: Can't.Two exams in between. History comes last.

SUSAN: It may be last...it will *not* be the *least!* Professor Woolsey doesn't kid around.

PAUL: I'm not kidding either. I've got to graduate. Y'know—my pop started saving for my college—on my first birthday! Same day we docked—coming over from the old country. Pop changed his last piece of European money into an American quarter—and started my college fund with it. [*Beat.*] I can't let 'em down, Mrs. Thornton. I'll graduate. *I have to.*

SUSAN: Yes, Paul.You have to.

[*She smiles at him encouragingly.*]

FADE OUT.

FADE IN: *Smoked glass door to* THORNTON'S *office. It is lettered*:

OFFICE OF THE PRESIDENT

DISSOLVE TO: *Office interior.* ALEX *hunches over his desk, adding and re-adding columns of figures. It's no use. With a groan, he crumples the sheet. Flings it away.*
SOUND: *Phone rings.*

ALEX: Thornton. [*Listens. Reacts*] Who? Are you *sure* it's Burton Bryce? *Of course* I'll see him! Right away! Thank you. [ALEX *stands, settles his tie, arranges papers on his desk. The door opens.* BURTON BRYCE *enters. He is a small man, deceptively mild; only occasionally do we glimpse the steely force of the bigot.* ALEX *coming forward*] Mr. Bryce? This is a pleasure . . . .

BRYCE: Dr. Thornton. Good of you to see me on such short notice. I don't come to town much any more. . . . Like to make a day count when I do. [*Beat.*] This is a busy season for you—eh?

ALEX [*nods*]: Commencements always fill me with mixed emotions. Relief, and regret too. I hate to see each class go.

BRYCE: Particularly—the class of '55, eh?

ALEX: I don't think I know what you—?

BRYCE [*cuts*]: Word gets around, Doctor. I keep to myself on my farm; but I make it my business to—know things! About to go broke here—right?

ALEX: Things are . . . tight.

BRYCE: What'd you expect? Small college—no endowment—high overhead? You don't charge enough tuition to keep in pencils! [ALEX *bridles.* BRYCE *waves a hand.*] I'm not criticizing you, Doctor. I've checked into your administration. It's okay. *You're* okay. [ALEX *gasps at this effrontery.*] But you're working on too small a scale.

ALEX: I resist the idea that only the titans can survive in this world.

BRYCE: Sure. You're a dreamer. That's okay. You're in the dream business here. Me—I'm a doer. I subsidize the dreams.

ALEX: I don't think I understand.

BRYCE: I've made a lot of money in my time. Now—I'm getting on. [*Pause. Huskily*] No one to leave it to. . . . Not—now. No one at all. . . . [*Then, crisply*] Fine crop of youngsters around here. Good pure-bred American stock. If they want to go to college—ought to have a college to go to!

ALEX: We're in complete agreement on that, sir!

BRYCE: All right then. Here's the proposition. I'm prepared to leave my entire fortune to Bradford College. And start the ball rolling with an immediate donation of three hundred thousand dollars!

[ALEX *gasps. Tries to speak. Can't. His shock and joy are too great. He sits abruptly. Tries to collect himself.*]

ALEX: I—I'm sorry... I—it's so wonderful... I don't know how to—

BRYCE: Discuss it with your trustees! Think it over a few days ... We'll make the public announcement at the Commencement exercises.

ALEX: Oh, yes! Yes! We'll want you on the platform... a presentation speech... all that ....

BRYCE: Good ... Sign all the papers right there. Kind of fitting. The end and the beginning—eh?

ALEX [*grabs* BRYCE'S *hand*]**:** God bless you, Mr. Bryce.

BRYCE: I'll get my lawyers to work ... drafting the papers. Er—just one more thing ... !

ALEX: Yes?

BRYCE: There's one condition. Little whim of mine. I want it understood—if Bradford College accepts my offer, it will *never* confer a degree on any person born on foreign soil.

[*A pause.* ALEX *gropes with the implications. Frowns.*]

ALEX: I want to be sure I heard you correctly. [*Slowly*] If we can't confer a degree ... what you're really saying is—you want all foreign-born students barred from Bradford College?

BRYCE: Er—yes. That's very well put. Beginning with the current class—your graduating class of '55! [*Beat.*] I'm a one hundred per cent American ... donating good, hard American cash, to educate the sons and daughters of Americans!

ALEX: America isn't a racial strain, Mr. Bryce! It's a way of life! A way of thought!

BRYCE [*a sneer*]**:** I've heard all that before! Listen ... [*Rising passion*] My son ... died like a *dog,* on a dirty foreign beachhead, fighting for riff-raff, too shiftless to fight for themselves! [*Hits it.*] You think I'd give one cent of my money to educate their brats?

ALEX [*taut*]**:** I can understand the reason for your prejudice, Mr. Bryce. But I can't permit the college to be a party to it! I'm sorry.

BRYCE [*slyly*]**:** I see. You think it's better... to have no college at all? [ALEX *winces. Bites his lip.*] Some school's going to accept this money. Some school's going to agree to my one little condition. Just remember—I came to you first. It could have been Bradford.

ALEX: How can you justify this stipulation in your own mind, sir? How do you explain it?

BRYCE: Why...the greatest good for the greatest number! You'll find that in Scripture, doctor. Story of the fishes and the bread that fed five thousand.

ALEX: All right. I concede—we'll be educating the multitude! But what about the kids, born abroad, who might want an education, too?

BRYCE: Just a minute. How many foreigners have entered Bradford in the six years you've been here?

ALEX: Er...let's see...One...two...three.... [*He counts sotto voce, as he thinks.*]

BRYCE [*triumphant*]: I thought so! Maybe one a year! Maybe none! How many in your senior class right now who are foreign born?

ALEX [*thinks*]: None. To my knowledge.

BRYCE: Are you going to turn down the chance to educate hundreds of students every year...because of one or two?

ALEX [*feebly*]: But—it's the principle of the—!

BRYCE [*scornfully*]: Pshaw! Where's your common sense, man? [*He pounds on desk.*] I'm offering you a chance to save this college, for good and all! Are you interested? Or—not?

ALEX [*struggle within...then*]: Yes...I'm interested. [*He sinks back in his chair, as if exhausted.* BRYCE *smiles, nods in satisfaction. Hauls up a chair, as we fade out.*]

> FADE IN: WOOLSEY'S *classroom. Same day. About an hour later.* PROF. WOOLSEY, *a gaunt, hawk-faced old man, stands behind his desk, which is heaped high with term papers.* PAUL, *sullen with rage, confronts him.* WOOLSEY *is chewing* PAUL *out over his paper, spread out on the desk. As he talks, he spears at the paper with a heavy black pencil.*

WOOLSEY [*venomously*]: Puerile! . . . Implausible! . . . Inconclusive! . . . Improbable! . . . Idiotic! . . . Careless! . . . Slipshod! . . . And *dull!* [*Gathers himself for the finale*] Mr. Rudolph, do you call this wretched example of sub-human intelligence...a *term paper!*

PAUL: Well, actually, sir . . . when I was writing it, I just called it . . . "The Horror."

> [WOOLSEY *gurgles in rage.*]

WOOLSEY: Your humor is abysmal! Your insolence is monumental!

121

You are, without doubt, the most annoying student I've encountered in 40 years of teaching! How long must I put up with this?

PAUL: Well, it's six more days till the 30th, sir. That's Commencement.

WOOLSEY: Don't tax your brain remembering the date. It will be a day, like every other day, for you! You will not pass History 4. Therefore you will not be graduating on Commencement Day.

[*He sits. Marks a huge "F" on* PAUL'S *paper. Shoves it at him. Busies himself with other papers.* PAUL'S *fury surges up like a wave.*]

PAUL: You're not getting away with this, Woolsey! I'm going to Thornton. I'll tell him what a miserable, mean—

[*Sound: Knock at open door.*]

ALEX [*steps in*]: Sorry to break in, Professor, I know this is your usual hour for interviewing students, . . . but—

WOOLSEY [*cuts, coldly*]: I am in the *middle* of the hour, Dr. Thornton. You know my feelings about routine.

ALEX: I'm calling an emergency meeting of the faculty, Professor Woolsey. I must insist on your attendance. We're meeting in my office, as soon as everyone can get there.

PAUL [*hastily*]: If you both will excuse me . . . ? Dr. Thornton. Professor—

[*He hurries out.* WOOLSEY'S *scowl relaxes, as soon as* PAUL *is gone.*]

WOOLSEY: That one's a handful! Needs a bridle! We had quite a set-to, when I—

ALEX [*cuts*]: We'll discuss Paul later! You've heard of Burton Bryce, the millionaire . . . ?

WOOLSEY [*tops him*]: Boy said he worked for you, and your wife. Very fond of both of you—

ALEX [*driven*]: Forget Paul for a minute! Please, Professor. Bryce has a proposition which can affect the future of the entire college . . . . [*He turns towards the door.*] Hurry along, would you?

WOOLSEY [*sotto*]: ". . . The future of the *college?*" [*He grunts.*] College is made up of *people! People!* They're the ones you're going to affect!

FADE OUT.

FADE IN: *Thornton living room. Same day. About 8 P.M.* SUSAN *is talking on phone. She is clearly confused and disturbed.*

SUSAN: There must be some mistake, Mrs. Winter. Dr. Thornton never mentioned a faculty meeting to me. [*Listens*] Oh . . . I see . . . [*Reacts.*] How much? [*A gasp.*] Three hundred thous—[*Listens. Reacts with disbelief.*] Alex is in favor—? I'm sorry . . . I simply can't believe . . . .

[SOUND: *Front door closes offstage.* ALEX *enters living room in time to hear last sentence or two. He is a man beset by conscience. He kisses the top of* SUSAN'S *head. Waits quietly for her to finish.*]

SUSAN [*goes on*]: . . . I don't want to doubt Professor Winter . . . but until Alex tells me himself—I—[ALEX *moves away quickly. Lights a cigarette.* SUSAN *watches him.*] He just came in, Mrs. Winter. Thank you for calling. Goodbye. [*She hangs up slowly. Turns to* ALEX.]

ALEX [*quickly*]**:** Every time I tried to phone—I got the busy signal. [*Brightly*] There's so much to tell, I don't know where to start!

SUSAN: I have a rough idea of what's gone on, from the faculty wives. [*Beat.*] I want you to tell me just one thing . . . .

ALEX: Let me explain everything point by point . . . .

SUSAN [*tops him*]**:** The rest doesn't matter! I want to know one thing, Alex! Do you want the college to accept Burton Bryce's offer?

ALEX: Susan, there are times when a man has to set aside his personal feelings!

SUSAN [*shouts*]**:** Answer me, Alex! Are you with Bryce? Or against him? [ALEX *cannot meet her eyes. He fumbles with his cigarette. Tries to appear cool and collected.*]

ALEX: If you insist upon taking the attitude that things are either black or white . . . right or wrong . . . then I will say . . . I am in favor of accepting his terms. [SUSAN *is speechless. She gives him a long, penetrating look, as if she is seeing him for the first time. Turns her back.* ALEX *moves closer to her.*] The real issue we are concerned with, Susan . . . is how can we save Bradford College, so the greatest number of students can benefit? No one will benefit if the college fails! Hundreds of young people . . . thousands over the years, can and will benefit if it stays open. Any injustice done to a few foreign-born students must be weighed against accomplishing a greater good for the majority!

SUSAN [*shocked*]**:** You make it all sound logical and reasonable, Alex! But the foreign-born students are human beings! You can't rationalize away their feelings!

ALEX [*smiles*]**:** That's the crux of the matter, Susan! There *are* no foreign-born students enrolled at Bradford now. That's why I agreed to Bryce's offer with a clear conscience. His stipulation exists in theory only.

SUSAN: You're wrong, Alex. Paul Rudolph was born in Europe. He told me so himself. If you accept Mr. Bryce's money, and his condition—you can't let Paul graduate from Bradford. [ALEX *stares at her, hypnotized. He can't seem to find words.*] What happens now, Alex? What are you going to do?

> [*He tries to speak. It's merely a groan. He claps his forehead. Goes to his desk. Stands there—trying to collect himself.* SOUND: *Doorbell.* SUSAN, *without a word, goes to door. It's* PROFESSOR WOOLSEY.]

WOOLSEY: Is he here? [SUSAN *nods. Gestures.* WOOLSEY *enters living room.* ALEX *instantly alerts.*]

ALEX: Hello, Woolsey. I was just on the point of phoning you. I didn't mean to be rude this afternoon when you spoke about Paul Rudolph!

WOOLSEY [*coldly*]: I thought it might interest you and Mrs. Thornton that he is failing History. [SUSAN *gasps.* Alex *reacts.*] He needs the credit to graduate, doesn't he?

SUSAN: Professor Woolsey . . . it's very important for Paul to get his diploma!

ALEX [*sternly*]: Susan!

SUSAN [*tops him*]: Can't he be coached . . . ? Or tutored?

WOOLSEY: It's very late for that . . . .

ALEX [*firmly*]: I suggest we let things take their course. Paul will almost certainly fail History. That automatically makes him ineligible for a degree. The situation is taken care of—and Paul's feelings aren't hurt.

SUSAN: How kind of you, Alex! How thoughtful . . . not to hurt his feelings!

WOOLSEY: Will somebody please explain—?

SUSAN: Paul is foreign-born, Professor Woolsey. It would be very embarrassing to Mr. Bryce and company if he were allowed to graduate.

WOOLSEY [*grimly*]: I see. [*He turns on* ALEX.] I came here to tell you that I am violently opposed to what you are doing. I had intended since I am retiring in one more week to keep my thoughts to myself. [*Beat.*] I have changed my mind! You can no longer distinguish

124

between integrity and expediency! I have watched you corrupt this college. I do not intend for you to make a mockery of it! I will oppose you, Thornton, with every breath in my body. I'll speak out against you as long and loud as I am able ... and I shall try, to the limit of my ability, to make sure that Paul Rudolph gets a degree from Bradford College on Commencement Day!

DISSOLVE.

ACT TWO

FADE IN: WOOLSEY'S *classroom. Night.* WOOLSEY *sits at desk, smoking. From offstage, chimes strike eight. He gets up nervously. Goes to door. Opens it. Peers cautiously into corridor. Closes door. Crosses to window, and carefully pulls a blind.*

SOUND: *Tap at door.*

PAUL [*offstage*]: Prof—?

WOOLSEY: Come in, Mr. Rudolph.

[PAUL *enters. Shuts the door. Collapses in chair. Cocks feet on corner of* WOOLSEY'S *desk. Sighs deeply.*]

PAUL: I'm bushed. I've fought from the War of the Roses, right up to the charge of the Light Brigade, since lunch.

WOOLSEY: Ummm. Excellent progress. I really feel much easier in my mind about you, Mr. Rudolph.

PAUL: I wish I felt easy in mine. It's like a rag-bag ... stuffed with a million odds and ends.

WOOLSEY: Well, now that you've accumulated all of them so diligently—forget them.

PAUL [*stares at him*]: Before the exam?

WOOLSEY: History is more than learning a thousand dates, and who fought where when, Mr. Rudolph. It isn't a static past. It's fluid ... like a river. You and I—sitting here—are the sum total of all the battles ... all the events and discoveries ... and the countless millions who have gone before us. A rebel slave of the Pharaohs contributed something to our freedom ... an Assyrian king dictated laws which influenced our courts. [*Beat.*] We are the history of tomorrow. If you compromise with injustice—others will suffer for it. If I do not speak out against prejudice ... tomorrow's sky may be black with it. [*Pause.*] That is the lesson for the day, Mr. Rudolph.

[Sound: *Knock at door.* Woolsey *stiffens.* Paul *looks puzzled.*]

ALEX [*O.S.*]: Are you there, Professor Woolsey? [Woolsey *sighs deeply. Goes to door.*]

WOOLSEY: Come in, Dr. Thornton. [Alex *enters. His gaze sweeps the room. He smiles to himself.*]

ALEX: I was passing and saw your light. You really should have told me you were giving Paul a refresher course. I might have sat in.

PAUL [*gets to feet*]: It's been darned interesting, Dr. Thornton. I feel I've learned a lot.

ALEX: So do we all, Paul. So do we all. [*Beat.*] Could I interrupt the study routine for a few minutes? I have something to say to Professor Woolsey.

PAUL: Certainly, sir. Excuse me.

[*He gathers books. Hurries out.* Alex *follows him to door. Carefully closes it. Faces* Woolsey.]

ALEX: I wouldn't have expected this of you, Woolsey.

WOOLSEY: I told you I would fight you.

ALEX: Just what do you expect to accomplish by furtively coaching Paul in the dark of night?

WOOLSEY: It's obvious, isn't it? I'm trying to insure the fact he'll pass his exam. In that case—you'll have to graduate him.

ALEX: But Professor Woolsey . . . you yourself are going to see to it—he does not pass! [Woolsey *laughs in his face.* Alex *is needled.*] We've played this little game long enough. Don't you realize you're jeopardizing your own future if this boy passes!

WOOLSEY: At the moment, I am more interested in Paul's future. And others like him.

ALEX: Give a little thought to your own, Professor! Your retirement becomes effective Commencement Day!

WOOLSEY: That is correct.

ALEX: I understand you plan to live on your retirement pay.

WOOLSEY [*nods*]: I have no savings to speak of. And at my age, I don't imagine I could find another teaching position.

ALEX: Then—isn't it to your own best interest to make sure Bradford College stays in business! [*Beat.*] If it folds, you will not draw retirement pay! You will be, to all effects, without funds! [*Pause.*] But if it remains open, you are taken care of.

WOOLSEY: You make the problem sound very simple, Dr. Thornton.

ALEX [*fiercely*]: It *is* simple. Bryce is adamant on the subject of foreigners! If we graduate a foreign-born student he will take his money and go elsewhere! The college will close. The faculty will be out of jobs. You yourself will be in a desperate situation.

WOOLSEY: You're appealing to my instinct of self-preservation.

ALEX: Can you think of a better one?

WOOLSEY: Yes. The instinct of truth. It is born in us—and from the moment of birth, man struggles to escape his awareness of it. He invents ways to hide from it. He substitutes reason. He appeals to common sense. He takes refuge in logic. He persuades himself that the end justifies the means. He commits terrible crimes—permits hideous injustices in his necessity to escape what cannot be escaped. But always—at some moment, some crisis—a man must face himself and the truth within him.

ALEX: I'm waiting for the revelation of this universal truth.

WOOLSEY: Why . . . it's very simple. We are all the same. We share humanity with every other living man. And no man is better than the next, under God. And no man is worse.

[*A pause.* ALEX *reacts. He is moved but unwilling to give in.*]

ALEX: Very astute, Professor Woolsey. Under your eloquent statement of equality and humanity, I recognize the attempt to save Paul Rudolph [*Beat.*] at the price of losing the college. *No!* [*He smashes his fist on the desk.*] I have committed myself to saving Bradford College. This is one case when rights of the individual will have to be sacrificed for the good of the many. Therefore, I shall accept your resignation—effective as of this minute! [WOOLSEY *reacts. He is stunned.*] I will make up a new history exam for Paul Rudolph, and give it to him myself. And I assure you—he will not pass it.

[ALEX *holds* WOOLSEY'*s gaze for a moment, until the old man bows his head, and sits heavily in defeat.*]

FADE OUT.

FADE IN: *Thornton living room in the evening.* SUSAN *stands at window, obviously watching for* ALEX. *Her face is drawn and troubled. She alerts—peers to make sure.*

SUSAN: He just turned the corner. He stopped to speak to Professor Winter. [*She turns from window to* PAUL, *who waits, grim-faced, in center of room.*] Paul . . . are you sure you want to do this?

PAUL: Yes.

SUSAN: I shouldn't have told you.

PAUL: Then I would have asked somebody else, Mrs. Thornton. And kept on asking till I got the [*Bitterly*] whole story. I'm not a fool, you know. It was obvious something was screwy when Dr. Thornton showed up this afternoon to give me the exam.

> [SOUND: *Door opens offstage.* SUSAN *starts to the hall, but* ALEX *enters. He carries a sheaf of exam books. Reacts when he sees* PAUL.]

ALEX: Well . . . hello, Paul. I didn't expect to see you quite so soon.

PAUL: I realize you haven't had time to check over my exam yet, sir.

ALEX: I know it's rough . . . sweating out the result . . . on the eve of Commencement. I'll get to it as soon as I can, and give you a call.

PAUL: That's all right, sir. It isn't necessary. [*Beat*] I—I came to tell you—I'm leaving tonight.

ALEX [*stunned*]: Leaving . . . ? Before you *know*—? I mean . . . I don't understand.

SUSAN: Paul wondered why Professor Woolsey did not give him his history exam, Alex. He asked me, and I told him.

ALEX [*horrified*]: You—?

PAUL: It's all right, sir. I realize what a spot you're in.

ALEX: Why, thank you, Paul. That's very—mature—of you. You understand that this whole thing . . . has nothing to do with you personally . . . ! If I had any other choice—

PAUL: Well . . . actually . . . if I leave—you won't have to make a choice at all. *Will you?*

ALEX: I don't understand.

PAUL: I've thought it all out, sir. Professor Woolsey was talking to me about compromise . . . and how it doesn't just affect me, or you. It seems to go on, and on. Like a river, he said. I've been here for four years, Dr. Thornton. And I know you're not the kind of man to compromise. If I pass that exam—you'd let me pass. Even though it'd mean closing the college and everything. I can't let that happen. It wouldn't be right. [ALEX *looks at* PAUL, *almost fearfully—as if his own conscience is facing him.* SUSAN *watches* ALEX . . . *hopefully . . . believing he will be forced to take a stand.*] I guess this is goodbye, sir. You and Mrs. Thornton have been swell to me. I feel I've learned a lot . . . from both of you. The kind of things you don't need a diploma for. [*He walks close to* ALEX.] You won't be wanting my exam now, sir. I'll take it with me.

ALEX [*an effort*]: If you don't mind, Paul . . . I'd like to keep it.

PAUL: Well . . . sure. It's up to you.

SUSAN: Goodbye, Paul. [*Beat.*] You make me . . . very proud.

> [*She embraces him.* PAUL *turns to* ALEX. *Puts out his hand.*
> ALEX *stares at it as if hypnotized.*]

PAUL: Thanks for everything, sir.

> [*Slowly,* ALEX *puts out his hand.* PAUL *shakes it. Walks quickly*
> *to the door. Exits.*]

SUSAN: How can you let him go, Alex? [*Vehemently*] How can you?

ALEX: Susan, please—don't start at me. I've had enough for one day.

SUSAN: Have you, Alex? Is it too much for you—being reminded that once you were a man of honesty and integrity? A man of no compromise? The kind of man who inspired the best in others—by setting the example?

ALEX [*urgently*]: Susan—!

SUSAN: Are you afraid if you hear the truth—you might have to face it? Face it now, Alex! Before it's too late! You can still call Paul back. You can still pass him! You can still hand him a diploma tomorrow morning!

ALEX [*violently*]: Are you crazy? It's settled! I'm not turning back now!

SUSAN: Then you will have to go on alone.

ALEX: What do you mean . . . ?

SUSAN: Each day I find I know you a little less. Until just now—when you let Paul go, I realized the man I loved is dead. I don't know you at all. I am married to a stranger.

> [*She turns and quickly exits.* ALEX *moves to stop her. He*
> *brushes against the stack of exam books he has put on*
> *the desk. They fall.* ALEX *stoops and picks them up. His*
> *gaze falls on* PAUL'S. *Slowly, reluctantly, drawn against his*
> *will, he sits, opens the book . . . and begins to read.*]
> FADE OUT.
>
> FADE IN: *President's office.* BURTON BRYCE *stands by the*
> *window looking out. If possible, we might see a student*
> *or so, through the window, in graduation robes and*
> *mortar boards.* BRYCE'S *assurance is monumental . . . he*
> *already owns the college. He turns as the door opens.*

129

WOOLSEY *enters, in robes. He looks surprised to see* BRYCE *... a little confused.*

WOOLSEY: Er ... I'm sorry. I was told Dr. Thornton wanted to see me.

BRYCE: Same here. Don't understand it at all. Ten minutes before the procession starts. They tell me I'm supposed to wear one of those things. Take me half an hour to get in it.

WOOLSEY: I beg your pardon. I don't believe I—

BRYCE: Why, I'm Bryce. Burton Bryce.

WOOLSEY: How do you do? My name is Woolsey.

BRYCE [*a start*]: Oh. [*Beat.*] You're leaving, I hear.

WOOLSEY: I'm retiring.

BRYCE: Sorry to hear it. Always admired a fellow with the courage of his convictions. Like people with grit. We might have had a couple of run-ins ... but that's healthy.

WOOLSEY: I'm afraid it goes a little deeper than that, Mr. Bryce.

[BRYCE *looks at him perplexedly.* ALEX, *in cap and gown, enters, followed by* SUSAN. *He carries* PAUL'S *exam book.*]

ALEX: I'm terribly sorry if I'm late. [*He exchanges a look with* SUSAN.] I was trying to catch a train before it left the station.

[SUSAN *smiles at* ALEX *faintly.*]

BRYCE: Well, let's get to it, Doctor. It's almost starting time. [*Chuckles.*] Don't want to miss my own party.

ALEX: I assure you, Mr. Bryce ... none of us will miss Commencement. [*He opens* PAUL'S *exam book.*] Here are the answers to an exam which I gave yesterday to a senior student, Paul Rudolph. I intended that Paul should fail the exam—to conform to your stipulation, Mr. Bryce that no foreign-born student should graduate from Bradford College.

BRYCE: Seems like a chancy thing to do, wait'll the last minute. . . .

ALEX: We only discovered the other day that Paul was born abroad. But I was taking no risk, I assure you. I was determined he should fail ... even if he wrote the most brilliant examination in the annals of education. [*Beat.*] Paul did *not* write a brilliant exam. I can criticize his knowledge of history. I cannot criticize his awareness of what it means to be a free citizen—free to seek learning, in a free state.

BRYCE: I can't make an exception, Doctor. Don't ask me to. Man's got certain principles. He's got to stick by them.

ALEX: I agree with you, Mr. Bryce. Bradford College has its principles too—and they aren't yours, and never can be. And I—thank God—have found mine again. I'm afraid there can be no conditions to learning, Mr. Bryce. Only if *all* of us . . . of whatever race or creed, or birth or belief, are free to seek and learn and discover . . . can we find truth.

BRYCE: Fine words, Doctor. Very pretty. But who's going to hear them? Who do you teach them to—if your college fails?

ALEX: Bradford won't fail. As long as there is one student to teach—we will find a place to teach him. [*From offstage we hear the processional hymn "Land of Hope and Glory," Elgar's "Pomp & Circumstance."*] Professor . . . we have some degrees to bestow. Perhaps you will be good enough to give Paul Rudolph his diploma.

> [WOOLSEY, *deeply moved, nods.* ALEX *opens the door—ushers the old professor out.* SUSAN *takes his arm, and together they exit. As the processional swells,* BRYCE, *a puzzled and rather shaken man, moves to the window. He stands, alone and forlorn—watching the gowned figures move off for the ceremony. Dissolve.*]

The Mountain

by Martin J. Hamer

The narrator remembers the time when he understood that some people would never see him clearly, no matter how close he was.

In the summer of 1943, Charlie was my best friend. We were in the same class in elementary school and we lived right next door to each other. He, in the first high stoop house from the corner, and I in the second. By standing on our backyard fire escapes and reaching out, we could pass things to one another. My mother came home late in the evening and my father never until much later, so when I came in from school, and my sister wasn't there to tell on me, I would climb out on the fire escape and call to Charlie. To do this, we each had a long string with a stone wrapped in cloth tied to it, hanging from our fire escapes. Once, when Charlie had been mean to the lady under him, she cut his string. Anyway, to call to each other, we would swing the stones so that they tapped the window.

The day of graduation from elementary school, Charlie was so excited when he came home that he almost broke my window. When

I climbed out on the fire escape, he was there all dressed up in his blue suit with a tragic look on his face.

"I thought you were dead," he said. "Why didn't you come to school?"

"I was sick," I answered.

"You don't look sick now...."

"How was it?" I interrupted.

"You didn't get left back, did you?"

"Of course I didn't."

"You know what somebody said?" he continued. "They said your mama couldn't afford to buy you a new suit."

"They were right."

"You mean you missed graduation because you didn't have a new suit?"

"Would you have gone if you didn't have one?"

"Yeah," he answered, "I guess you're right. I probably wouldn't have ... It's all that stupid principal's fault. If he hadn't announced that everybody had to wear blue suits and all that, this wouldn't have happened ...."

Then as an afterthought he added, "Couldn't your mama afford to buy you a new suit?"

"I don't know," I replied. "I guess not."

But really I didn't know. We weren't any poorer than Charlie's family, and from the way Mama had explained it when I had asked her, I had been unable to figure out whether we could afford it or not.

She had said that the Sunday suit I had was good enough for anybody's graduation, and that if any of the other kids were getting new ones, she hoped it was because they needed them. When I tried to explain that it wasn't the other kids I was thinking of, but my teachers, she looked at me real hard and said, "I *know* you don't want a new suit because the white man says so!"

"My principal says we should all ...."

"Your principal, huh? A hundred boys sitting up there in blue suits may be the most important thing in the world to him, but it's not to me. If how you look is all that counts then maybe you'd better stay home."

"But Mama, I can't stay home," I cried.

"Then go in what you got!"

I stared at her, unable to believe this lack of understanding, then turned and walked away.

I was sitting at the fire escape window indulging in a fantasy of how I would kill myself and she would have to buy the new suit to bury me in, when I felt her come up behind me.

"Look here," she said, "I want to talk to you." I dragged myself around, and saw her standing there wiping her hands in her apron.

"Honey," she began softly, "a new suit isn't going to change you as far as the white man is concerned. To him you'll still be a little colored boy . . . ."

"That man," she continued, looking off out of the window, "is up there on a mountain, and he'll probably be up there all your life . . . but remember, you're as good as he is, new suit or no new suit."

Tears began to run down my cheeks, but I gave no sign of even noticing them. She didn't understand me, my own mother. Here she was talking about mountains, and all I wanted was a new suit.

"Did you hear what I said?"

The tears came faster, and finally unable to ignore them, I wiped my shirtsleeve across my face, and blurted out, "All I want is a new suit!" Just then, the door opened and Daddy came in. When Mama turned around, I ran off.

I didn't tell Charlie any of this that day on the fire escape, and it wasn't until August that I realized what she meant. In August, Charlie and I decided to visit Columbia University. We planned the trip one day in advance, and the following morning arose very early and set out through Morningside Park, which separated the valley where we lived, from the area where the university lay. The park, a two block wide strip of trees, grass, rocks, and sand, rose steeply to Morningside Heights. Its many planned paths and beaten trails having long since given up their secrets to us, we crossed it rapidly, pausing only twice. Once to cautiously inspect a man who was lying in the bushes; we thought we had accidentally stumbled onto a murder, but it turned out he was a drunk. And the other time to throw stones at two dogs to prevent them from doing what we had been told would be injurious to their health.

At the top, we rested in an oval from where we could look out over the whole of Harlem. It was bunched up, it seemed, between Central Park and the Yankee Stadium, its old buildings spilling almost into the

East River with cars and people filling the remaining spaces like black lava. We tried to count all the parked cars we could see but, after reaching two hundred, we tired, turned, and headed toward the university.

We found ourselves in another world. The buildings were tall and immaculate, their polished brass fronts opening onto glistening tile floors which beckoned towards cool dark opulent depths. Awnings everywhere. And the streets were large and clean, the white granite faces of the buildings meeting the sidewalks in a line unbroken from corner to corner. After two blocks, we came to a sprawling group of buildings and Charlie said, "This must be it."

We stood, two small dark boys, before the Taj Mahal, before the Parthenon, and the Sphinx of Egypt. We stood, two small dark boys, before the reality of our dreams. There were steps of stone that ran for almost a block, with lions, one at either end, from which a king might speak, and red bricks where girls in veils could dance before a great feast. And a pool. And tennis courts. And flagstone walks, that led through gardens with benches hewed from stone by slaves. We climbed the stairs, stood before the doors, and read the inscription carved there in the stone: "The Low Library, Columbia University."

Then we continued westward to the Hudson River and south along Riverside Drive, finding ourselves by four in the afternoon in Columbus Circle. With our last bit of change we paid our subway fare for the ride home. The trains were crowded, and Charlie and I were pressed up against the doors hardly able to breathe as the express left 59th street. We were grinning at each other, our day having been filled with wonders that only we two shared, when the lady in front of me suddenly looked down, saw that her purse was open, fumbled around inside it for a moment; then turned to me and said, "Little boy, give me back my wallet!" All noises ceased. All except the roar of the fans. "Little boy, please give me back my wallet!" All pressures ceased. The surrounding bodies moving away from us. All except the pressure of shame and humiliation that came with her words. I finally replied, "I haven't got your wallet, Miss."

The train rushed on towards 125th Street. A man pushed his way to the front of the crowd. The woman repeated her plea. And Charlie and I stood, our hands locked together, their perspiration forming a bond that was our only salvation.

135

It takes seven minutes for the express to travel between 59th Street and 125th Street. After five of those minutes, the man offered to search us. The woman, busily searching her purse, either did not hear him or did not care to commit herself. Seconds later, she found her wallet—in her purse.

She apologized. And the man, feeling perhaps even more ashamed, reached into his pocket, brought out a half dollar, and tried to press it into Charlie's hand. Water reached the crotch of Charlie's trousers, chose the left leg, coursed its way down his thigh, across his knee, into his socks, over his shoe, and puddled at its tip. And my shame gave way to anger as it grew in size. I raised my head, looking directly at no one, but into the crowd and said, "No thank you mister. No thank you."

That evening we met on the fire escape. We passed things to each other for a while and then Charlie said, "Some trip today, huh?" I was staring off towards the park and didn't answer. "Yeah," he continued, "that was some trip . . . . You know what? I bet if we had been dressed up, I bet that woman wouldn't have thought we robbed her."

"Yes she would have, too," I replied. "It wouldn't have made any difference."

"How do you know it wouldn't have made any difference?" I almost told him what Mama had said, but changed my mind.

"I just do, that's all . . . I just do."

We stood looking at each other; I'm sure he knew what I meant. Then two cats began fighting in the backyard, we turned to watch, and night fell.

Dirge Without Music

by Edna St. Vincent Millay

I am not resigned to the shutting away of loving hearts in the hard ground.
So it is, and so it will be, for so it has been, time out of mind:
Into the darkness they go, the wise and the lovely. Crowned
With lilies and with laurel they go: but I am not resigned.

Lovers and thinkers, into the earth with you.
Be one with the dull, the indiscriminate dust.
A fragment of what you felt, of what you knew,
A formula, a phrase remains,—but the best is lost.

The answers quick and keen, the honest look, the laughter, the love,—
They are gone. They are gone to feed the roses. Elegant and curled
Is the blossom. Fragrant is the blossom. I know. But I do not approve.
More precious was the light in your eyes than all the roses in the world.

Down, down, down into the darkness of the grave
Gently they go, the beautiful, the tender, the kind;
Quietly they go, the intelligent, the witty, the brave.
I know. But I do not approve. And I am not resigned.

The Boy Next Door

by Ellen Emerson White

The people you've known your entire life can be very different from what you imagine. Behind their everyday faces might lie frightening fantasies. The author of this story establishes a matter-of-fact mood early on, and then depends on that mood to achieve the final effect.

Winter, in New England, was much too cold for ice cream. But the show must go on, the store must stay open, and Dorothy was working from four to nine. The closing shift. It was boring to work by herself, but they weren't getting enough business for her boss to justify paying extra staff.

It was *very* boring.

A few parents—divorced fathers, mostly—brought their kids for pre-bedtime cones; some sorority girls from the university rushed in to get a cake for a birthday that had been forgotten. She talked them into the 12-inch, instead of the 9, because—they were supposed to sell up. When someone asked for a cone of chocolate chip, or whatever, she was supposed to say, "Yes, sir, would that be a medium?" Because suggesting a *large* cone would make customers nervous, and inclined to say, "No, no, just a small." But "medium" sounded so—so *harmless.* So average.

138

The same way $1.99 sounded so much less expensive than $2.

As memory served, W.C. Fields had a theory about that.

Two couples came in, double-dating. The girls were, quite vocally, watching their weights, so they decided on small diet Cokes. The guys didn't seem too happy about that, and there was a lot of discussion before all four of them finally ordered sundaes. "No nuts on mine," one of the girls added, quickly, which would be a not-inconsiderable saving in calories, considering that they were butter-toasted—but a rather paltry saving, in the scheme of the overall sundae.

Dorothy, however, just kept her mouth shut, and made the sundaes. Rang them up. Gave back the change. Rinsed the two scoops she'd used.

Business was slow, and dull. Although there were worse things than getting paid minimum wage for doing physics homework.

Around 7:30, her friend Jill came in. Best friend, actually. They had met in kindergarten, and become instantly inseparable because they were the only two in the class who could read, and looking at d-o-g and c-a-t flashcards was dull. "Ennui," Jill had said, more than once. "Our friendship is *founded* on ennui."

Not that she had a flair for the dramatic or anything.

In many ways, they were exact opposites—Jill was tall, she was short; Jill was blonde, she had dark hair; Jill liked art, she liked science—but by the time they had got around to noticing that they had very little in common, they were already such close friends that it didn't matter.

"So," Jill said, leaning heavily against the counter. "What do I get free?"

Dorothy grinned and pointed in the direction of the drinking fountain.

"Think I'll pass," Jill said and took off her mittens. Lumpy looking mittens, but then again, she'd made them herself, and Dorothy had to give points for that. "It's really *cold* out—are people actually coming in here?"

Dorothy shook her head. "No."

Jill hung over the glass counter, looking at the various tubs. "Is that one new?" she asked, pointing.

"Yeah, Licorice." Dorothy reached for a little wooden paddle. "Want to try it? It's even worse than Pumpkin."

Jill tasted a spoonful, then nodded. "It's almost as bad as Cinnamon Crunch."

Dorothy nodded, took the paddle back, and threw it away.

Jill unzipped her jacket slightly, then zipped it back up. "I was kind of surprised there were so many people," she said.

The funeral. "Small town," Dorothy said. Almost everyone knew everyone else, so when someone died—or was born—or played Little League—or had a yard sale—a lot of people showed up. So even though Mrs. Creighton had been an absolutely *terrible* teacher—a complete terror, when you got right down to it—the church had been packed. The funeral had been over the weekend—but that didn't mean that everyone wasn't still talking about it.

"Yeah," Jill said and frowned. "I'm just always surprised. I mean, no one likes you while you're alive, but then you *die,* and suddenly, everyone's lining up to give eulogies. It's strange."

Dorothy nodded. Very strange.

"I really don't *like* funerals," Jill said.

Dorothy nodded. No argument there.

"Well." Jill straightened up. "Think you'll get out of here in time for 'Miss America'?"

Dorothy looked around the empty store. "Unless I get a rush."

"Right." Jill grinned, and also looked around. "Well, if you do, come by, or call me up—I have a feeling it's Miss Rhode Island's year."

Highly unlikely. "I'm going with the Pacific Northwest," Dorothy said. Miss—Oregon, maybe. Not that she had any real idea of what any of the contestants looked like. Or, really, even cared much.

"Not a chance," Jill said. "Unless they have really good talent." She paused. "I can't remember why we wait all year to watch it."

Well—not for the baton twirling. "Because we each, secretly, want to be Miss Congeniality," Dorothy said.

"Oh. Right." Jill put her mittens back on and headed for the door. "Don't work too hard."

Dorothy nodded and, finished with her physics homework, reached for her calculus book.

The store manager, Howard, stopped by at 8:30, to grumble about the lack of money in the register, and take most of it back to the safe. Then he came back out to remind her about turning off the heat under the hot fudge and butterscotch, being sure to rotate the ice-cream sandwiches when she restocked, and to remember to turn on the alarm system before she left.

She nodded, already at work refilling the jimmies. Sprinkles. Ants. Everyone who came *in* had a different name for them.

By the time she'd locked up, promptly at nine o'clock, she only had to tip the chairs up on top of the tables, mop the floor, and spray-clean the glass on the display cases.

Howard hated fingerprints. Small children sometimes even left *face* prints.

It was ten after nine when someone knocked on the door. She pointed to the CLOSED sign, then saw that it was Matt Wilson—whom she had known since third grade. They had even gone on a date—once—to the movies. Freddy Krueger. Not exactly her idea of a thrill, although Matt had liked it just fine. She had kissed him, pleasantly, good night, and since then, they had treated each other with mutual, vague disinterest. Had some of the same classes, ended up at the same football parties, said hi if they ran into each other at the mall. Other than that, they rarely spoke.

She didn't particularly want to let him in—but if she didn't, it was the sort of thing that would get around school, and everyone would think she was a—do you really *care* what people think, Jill would say. And she would probably answer that she did more than she didn't.

Besides, it was pretty cold out there.

"Hi," she said, unlocking the door. "I kind of have to close up."

Matt nodded, coming in. Since she remembered him as a skinny 10-year-old in maroon Toughskins jeans, it was always sort of a shock to realize that he was six feet tall now, had a much deeper voice—and possibly even shaved. Hard to believe it was the same guy who had thrown up on the bus—all *over* the bus—when they had gone on a field trip to the aquarium in the sixth grade.

"You want anything?" she asked. "Before I finish scooping down?" She went back behind the counter—and back to the Chocolate Walnut Fudge, which was frozen rock-solid and unyielding.

"They make you work alone?" he asked.

"Well—we aren't exactly thriving lately," she said, gesturing toward the empty parking lot. Well, empty except for her parents' station wagon.

Matt nodded, looking around. Shifting his weight from one high-top to the other. Looking around some more.

Call her prescient, but she was getting a bad feeling here. "Uh, Matt?" she said. "I can make you something fast, but then I really have to lock up."

Now he looked at her, and—his eyes seemed a little funny. Too bright, or—too *something*. Jumpy. "I want to see what it's like," he said, quietly.

Make that a *very* bad feeling. "Oh, yeah?" she said. "The thing is, my manager's going to show up, and if you're in here, I'm going to get in trouble."

He shook his head.

"Come on." She started to move out from behind the counter again. "I don't want to lose my job."

He shook his head. "I saw him. He already left."

He'd been watching. Great. And her car was the only one out there, so he must have parked somewhere else. Must have been *planning* this. Whatever it was.

She glanced down at the little metal ice-cream spatula she was holding—it wasn't much, as weapons went—then glanced in the direction of the wall phone. A good 15 feet. And it had a *dial*, not push buttons, so it would take her longer to get an operator.

Well, gosh.

Time to be distracting. After all, she'd known the guy since *third grade*. How dangerous could he really be? "Matt, if you don't take off," she said, "I'm never going to make it home in time for 'Miss America.'"

He just looked at her.

"And—neither are you," she said.

He didn't say anything.

Keep talking. "Well, okay, I see your point," she said, nodding. "You've probably already missed the swimsuits."

He looked at her with very little expression. Slight eagerness, maybe. "Open the register."

She stared at him. "What?"

"*Open* the register," he said.

This was scary—but this was also weird. "What do you mean?" she asked. "There's almost nothing in there. No one buys ice cream in weather like this."

"*Open* the damn register," he said.

"Oh, and give you the whole 20 dollars?" she asked. "If there's even that much."

His fist came out, unexpectedly, and knocked the glass donation jar off the counter. It landed with a shattering crash, change rolling all over the floor. Which was scary, but it made her a little mad, too.

"That's for crippled children," she said. "You really going to take money from *crippled children?*"

He looked at her with the same strange—blank—expression.

"On top of which," she said, "I *just* swept."

He came over the counter with an easy athletic motion, landing right in front of her. And, under the circumstances, it occurred to her that six feet was pretty big. A good 10 inches—and at least 80 pounds—bigger than she was.

The small metal spatula probably wasn't going to tip the odds.

Not that it wouldn't be worth a try. But—she would keep it as a trump card.

"Matt, this is really weird," she said. "Are Nicky and Fred and all those guys outside, and you're all just pulling my leg here? Because I *really* want to close up."

He reached into his jacket pocket—expensive Goretex—and brought out a gun. A handgun. Which he pointed at her. "I want to know what it's like," he said.

Well, this was just going from bad to worse, wasn't it. "Why don't you help yourself to the twenty," she said, indicating the register. "Take the money for Muscular Dystrophy, too. In fact," she pulled a five-dollar bill out of her jeans, "take this. Get yourself a couple of Big Macs."

He didn't even seem to hear that, holding the gun, and smiling slightly. "I've *always* wanted to know what it's like," he said. This had moved beyond weird, past ominous, and straight to dire. The thing to do, was stay calm. "I don't know, Matt," Dorothy said, putting the five-dollar bill back. "This is turning into a bad *Afterschool Special,* know what I mean?"

Since he was just standing there, smiling—he probably didn't know what she meant.

Okay. Time to go into a holding pattern. Since she *really* wasn't enjoying looking at a gun that might—might not?—be loaded. "Well," she said. "I think I'll—"

He stuck the gun into the back of her uniform shirt. "I think you'll shut up."

Okay. She shut up.

"I'll take the money," he said, and twisted the spatula out of her hand. It fell into the ice cream case, out of reach. "After. To make it look like a robbery."

"Okay," she said, checking the quiet street outside. Since everything was closed, there wasn't much reason for anyone to drive by. Even one of the few town police cars. "But you'd better hurry, because my father's going to be coming to pick me up."

He jabbed the gun into her back, then pointed with it at her car, out in the snowy parking lot.

"I know," she said. "Dead battery."

He jabbed her, harder, with the gun. "Shut up."

Well—it had been worth a try. She shrugged, and shut up. There was going to be a point at which she was going to have to take this situation a little more seriously—start *panicking*—but she wasn't there yet. This was, after all, a guy who had always tried, and failed, to cheat off her in eighth-grade earth science.

"I'm going to kill you," he said.

There it was—her cue to take this seriously.

"See"—his smile widened a little—"I've always wondered what it would be like—you know, to kill someone—so, I'm going to do it. Find out. And the police'll just think it's a robbery, see?"

Unh-hunh. She edged a step away from him.

"I really want to. Always have," he said. "I've been thinking about it for a long time, and—you know, what it would *feel* like—and I think—" He grinned, a little. "I've been planning this, you know?"

Well—she certainly knew now. "Boy," she said, keeping her voice calm, "and people say it isn't dangerous for MTV to show all those violent images."

He didn't seem to think that was funny. Somehow, she wasn't surprised.

"Look, I don't know if you're kidding, Matt," she said, "but, either way, I think you should consider *intensive* psychotherapy."

He didn't seem to think that was funny, either.

"Okay if I sit down for a minute, Matt?" she asked. "Considering how long we've known each other?"

"Sure." He laughed again. "We got at least 30 minutes, an hour, I figure, before anyone thinks it's funny the lights are still on in here."

It would probably be that long before her parents got worried enough to call, or show up. They didn't like the idea that she closed up alone, on weeknights. They were always afraid that something—bad—might happen.

In the future, she was going to have to take those sorts of concerns more seriously.

"On the floor," he said. "So no one will see us if they go by. Right there." He indicated for her to sit down against the counter, and then he sat down too, looking pleased with himself, his back resting against the soft-ice-cream machine.

Her head hurt, in a numb sort of way. "Want a dish of Cinnamon Crunch?" she asked. "It's really good."

He scowled at her. "You'd better start being scared. It's not as fun if you're not scared."

Exactly. She resisted the urge to rub her temples. "So, if you're a robber, how'd you get in? Would I really have opened the door?"

He gestured with the gun. "I'll break the glass, on my way out."

Oh. "Wouldn't I have heard you?" she asked.

"I'll turn the radio up," he said.

Oh.

"See," his eyes brightened even more, "it looks *fun*. When they do it. When you see films of it, and all. So, I want to see what it's like. To do it."

What had he been doing, sitting at home watching reenactments on *America's Most Wanted*? Taping shows like that so he could watch them over and over? He seemed so normal, the neighbors would say. So polite. The boy next door. "Shouldn't you work your way up?" she asked. "Start off by—I don't know—throwing rocks at sea gulls?"

He smiled. "I killed a dog."

Oh. She rubbed her hand across her forehead. Thought thoughts about aspirin.

"But, you know, I didn't *feel* anything," he said. "I didn't feel good, or bad, or—maybe, 'cause I used a car. Maybe if I'd really *done* it, myself, I—so I'm really going to *do* this. And—then I'll know."

The thing she had to keep in mind here, was that Matt Wilson wasn't exactly the brightest guy she had ever known. So—keep him talking. "Did we really have *that* bad a time on our date?" she asked.

He didn't say anything, just stood there, looking at her, holding the gun with great confidence. Familiarity. Pleasure.

Well, "Quick on the uptake" wasn't going to go on *his* tombstone. "I don't want to be trite," she said, "but, why me?" Such a nice boy, the elderly neighbor would tell Maury Povich. Always shoveled my walk.

"Because—you're not special," he said.

Oh. Not exactly the answer she had expected. Her breath got stuck somewhere inside her throat, and it was an effort to swallow.

"You know what I mean?" he said, leaning forward. "You're just— you're just *there*. Like, I know you, and I see you around, but—I don't give you any thought. Like, if you *weren't* there, I don't think I'd really notice." He frowned. "I don't think anyone really will. After the first couple weeks, or—maybe not even *that* long. You know?"

"The feeling's mutual," she said stiffly. Nice to have her entire existence reduced to a footnote. A Memorial Page in the yearbook. *If* that.

"Like," he didn't even seem to hear her, too far into his own crazed little reverie, "they'll be sad, at school, at *first,* and they'll have, you know, counselors come, so everyone can *talk* about how sad they are, and then—" he snapped his fingers. "Next thing you know, spring training'll be starting."

The fact that he just might be right was almost more terrifying than the rest of this. People's lives *were* getting pretty disposable these days. Even if you died in a really *interesting* way, you *still* might not make the evening news.

"So, I do you," he said, "and—big deal. They shouldn't've had you working here alone at night. 'Cause—you got robbed by some hopped-up junkie with a"—he made his hand shake on the gun— "quick trigger finger."

He *had* been thinking about this. What a waste of limited brain power. Because—it *would* look like a robbery gone bad. Like her mother always said, plenty of bad things happen in small towns, not just big cities, but the difference was, in the small town, you *knew* the people.

Her head hurt. She wanted to go home. The floor was filthy. "What about fingerprints?" she asked.

He grinned. "Haven't touched a thing. And if I do have to—" With his free hand, he took a pair of winter gloves out of his pocket to show her.

"Well." She leaned back against the cold white counter. There was a small chocolate smudge, maybe knee-high. "That's good. You've thought of—almost everything."

"I've thought of *everything*," he said, and glanced at his watch. "I want you to lie down now. Hands behind your head."

Oh, great. Execution-style. He must have been renting gangster movies. It was important to keep in mind that she really was smarter than he was. Maybe not *special*, but definitely smarter. "What you haven't thought about," she said, "is what it's *really* like to kill someone. It *is* easy, but it's pointless. Even if it's personal."

He scowled at her. "Shut up. I'm getting tired of you."

"Yeah, but"—she lowered her voice, carefully, as though there were someone else around to hear—"I know what I'm talking about."

He scowled at her, but uneasily.

Okay, good. Keep it up. "Even if the person probably *should* die," she said. "Even if you have a *serious* grudge against them, it doesn't seem to matter. Because, it doesn't change anything. You do it, and you don't feel better, you just feel—nothing. Like the dog. You feel—it's a waste. You risk so much, and you don't get anything back."

"What do *you* know about it?" he asked—but at least he was listening.

Okay, she'd got his attention. Time to bring out the big guns. "I know more than you think," she said. "But—we have to have a deal. If I tell you, you have to leave here, and no one'll ever know about this. Because we'll each have something to hold over each other, so—we can just keep it to ourselves."

He frowned at her suspiciously. "You just don't want me to kill you."

God, he was dense. "Well, *obviously*," she said. "Would I really be stupid enough to tell you about this, otherwise?"

He frowned. Pointed the gun. "Tell me what?"

Dorothy took a deep breath, then let it out. "I killed Mrs. Creighton."

He sat up straighter, then shook his head. "Oh, yeah, *right*. Nice try. You're just like, *stalling*."

No, she was trolling her line out, trying to get him hooked. "You want to hear what it was like?" she asked. "Stuff *nobody* else knows?"

He didn't say yes, but she could tell he was starting to get a little curious. Intrigued.

"Think about it, Matt," she said. "We were all in her class together." Fifth grade. "Think about what a terrible teacher she was. She was really *mean* to me—remember?"

He frowned. "No. Like, she was mean to everyone."

"Yeah, well, I didn't like it." She paused. For great effect. "And I waited a *long* time to get back at her."

It was quiet for a few seconds, the hum of the freezers sounding loud.

"She was in an accident," Matt said. "Just a dumb accident on the ice."

Dorothy nodded. "That's right. I *wanted* it to look like an accident. The same way you want *this* to look like an accident." Hooked? Or still just nibbling at the bait?

He glanced at his watch, then looked back at her, grinning. "Okay," he said. "Let's see how far you can take this, hunh?"

Hooked. "First, promise not to tell anyone," she said.

He laughed. "Like I'm really going to tell anyone what you *said* while I was *killing* you?"

Okay, so she wasn't making as many inroads as she'd thought. "I'm not kidding, Matt," she said. "I'm making a deal here. And—admit it. You want to hear about it."

"I'm the one holding the gun," he said. "*I'm* the only one who can make deals."

"Fine." She folded her arms across her chest. "Go ahead and shoot. Before you run out of time."

He shook his head, looking very amused. Stupidly amused. "No. I want to hear about your big-wow murder plot, first."

Well, it was the only hand she had, so she might as well play it out. Go for broke. "You know how the road curves there?" she said. Everyone in *town* knew about that curve. "Above the ocean? And that's the way she would *have* to drive. To get home. And, well, I know what her car looks like, right? Same way you know that's my parents' car out there in the parking lot."

He frowned, but he *was* still listening.

148

No matter what a story was about, the important thing was to tell it well. With *conviction.* "So I waited," she said. "In the bushes, there, just around the curve. More than one afternoon, if you want to know the truth. Because—she had to go by—and I figured the best time was right after dusk."

He shook his head, scornfully—but didn't, she noticed, interrupt.

"So no one would see me, and so she wouldn't have time to react." She was getting a little stiff, and would have stretched, but didn't want to do anything to distract him. "It's a funny thing about that curve," she said. "It really is dangerous, but everyone always drives pretty fast around it. I guess because they know it's there, and don't think about it much. I mean, *I* go fast around that curve, don't you?"

He nodded, then frowned, and pointed the gun.

Play it out. "So I waited," she said. "I had a pretty good view, because I wanted to be able to see her coming in plenty of time. And I was trying to think, how could I be *sure* she would turn out of the way fast? Be *sure* she'd go right over on to the rocks there."

He wasn't looking at her now, so much as *watching* her.

"Because—I was only going to get one chance," she said.

He watched her.

"A baby carriage," she said. And paused. "I don't care who you are, no matter where you are—even if it doesn't make sense—if you see a *baby carriage* come out in front of your car, you're going to try not to hit it. Right? Makes sense, doesn't it?"

Matt nodded a little.

"Right," she said. Press on. "So I waited. And I waited. And Thursday afternoon, right after dark, *who* should come speeding along?" She paused, then nodded significantly. "Yeah. So I timed it. Wanted to be sure she'd *see* it, but only after it was too late. I *timed* it, and then I pushed the carriage out there, and—" She let herself grin with exquisite slowness. "And she swerved, and went *right off the road,* just like I thought she would."

Matt was watching her with his mouth hanging open, although he probably wasn't aware of it.

Good. Keep going. "I didn't bother looking down over what was left of the guardrail," Dorothy said. "In case she *hadn't* been killed, and only—maimed—or something, and was looking up. I just went out to the middle of the road, got the baby carriage, and carried it back, through the bushes, to my car, so I could get rid of it." She paused. Slightly longer than briefly. "Evidence—right?"

She checked Matt's expression; he was frowning.

"But, here's the problem," she said. "The problem for you. I *really* didn't like her. I had it *in* for her. And yeah, she ran off the road, and yeah, it was because of me, and—it didn't seem to matter. It wasn't a kick. It was just like, so what? I mean, you're right—you and I have absolutely no opinion about each other. So, if you *waste* it on me, take the chance, it's just—stupid. If you have to do it, make it someone you *hate*. Try to make it worth your time and trouble. Make it worth the *risk*."

It was quiet again.

"Nice story," he said, then cocked the gun. "Now, put your hands behind your head."

She'd really thought she'd had him going along there. "I can *prove* it," she said, as he started to get up.

He stopped.

"Because"—keep that brain working quickly—"even when you're sure you've thought of everything, you haven't."

He eased back down, but kept the gun cocked. "So prove it."

"She *hit* the carriage," Dorothy said. "So if the police or, I don't know, whoever, checked the bumper, they'd find paint or metal chips that *weren't* from the guardrail."

He shrugged. "So?"

Slap down the last card. Full force. "I'll tell you where the carriage *is*," she said. "So if I went to the police, and said you came in here and threatened me, *you* could easily tell them I was lying about it, because you knew about Mrs. Creighton."

He narrowed his eyes at her.

"It's *perfect*," she said. "This way, we're both off the hook. We can both go home and—pretend this never happened."

"Yeah, right," he said. "Like I'm going to fall for *that*."

Yes. He was. "I threw it off the bridge," she said. "Up near the Point? Because, even when the tide goes out, and it's just marshy, there's so much junk down there, I knew no one would notice."

He frowned, but indecisively. "I know you're lying."

"We can drive up there," she said. "After school tomorrow. I can *show* you." She almost had him here—she could feel it. So she paused

150

again. "And, if you want," she paused again, "I'll tell you about the others."

There was no question but that his eyes widened. "The *others?*"

Hook, line, *and* sinker. "Seems to me," she said, "that there's been more than one accident in this town, in the last couple of years." Remember to pause. "I can tell you all about them."

"I *know* you're lying," he said, but without much assurance.

She shook her head. "No, you don't. Admit it. You know I'm telling the truth."

He looked at her. *Studied* her.

"You know I am," she said quietly.

There was another long silence, and then, finally, he nodded.

Next stop, National Poker Championships. "Yeah," she said. "I'll tell you about all of them, and then—maybe you and I can do another. *Together.*"

He looked at her. Started to grin.

"What the hell," she said. "Maybe it would be more fun that way. If you had someone to *share* it with."

The phone rang, suddenly, and they both jumped.

"What's that?" he asked nervously.

She checked her watch. "My parents. Because I'm running late."

The phone rang again.

"Look, get out of here," she said. "You can't do anything now, because they'll *know* it wasn't a robber. Get out of here, and we can talk at school tomorrow."

The phone had rung again, and then again.

"*Go,*" she said. "Don't be stupid."

A fifth ring.

He nodded, getting up, and she got up, too, answering the phone. Indeed, her mother.

"Oh, hi, Mom," she said. "Yeah, I was down in the basement, getting straws and napkins and all." She motioned toward the door, and Matt nodded.

"Tomorrow?" he said.

She nodded; *he* nodded; and he left.

Left.

All right! Nice *talking,* Tex.

She explained to her mother that she was still cleaning up, was almost done, and got permission to stop by Jill's to watch the end of "Miss America." Then, once she'd hung up, she went over and locked the door. Took the keys, and put them in her pocket. Lowered the lights.

She should probably call the police—or have told her mother, but—tell them what? That the right tackle on the football team suffered from psychosis? Had a violent fantasy life? Was just plain wacko? That he'd broken the Muscular Dystrophy jar? That he had—all she wanted to do right now was get out of here. Then she could worry about how to handle the situation.

She swept up the glass and pennies. Left a note for Howard that the jar had fallen, and put the change in an empty box that had once held cans of whipped cream. She took up the chairs, mopped the floor, turned the lights off, and the alarm *on.*

It was 10:15. Seemed later.

She went out to the parking lot, and sat in the car. Sat, taking deep breaths, seeing her hands still shaking with reaction trembling.

That had been scary. Really, really *scary.* Unbelievable in fact. And—she wasn't quite sure what to do. If she should just go home, or—she started the car, and pulled out of the parking lot, driving slowly and cautiously, on the ice. Headed toward Jill's house.

Jill's little brother, Timmy, let her in.

"You're late," he said cheerfully. "You missed the question-and-answer section."

Dorothy nodded. "Yeah, I know. She in the den?"

"Yup," he said, and offered her his bag of Doritos.

"No, thanks," she said, and headed for the den.

Jill was sitting in there, alone, wearing her reading glasses, her French book open—and completely ignored—on her lap. "Hi," she said.

Dorothy nodded, and sat down in the easy chair.

"Miss Nebraska had a really nice gown," Jill said.

Dorothy nodded, trying to figure out exactly how to explain what had happened tonight. Exactly what to say.

"But her hair was stupid." Jill glanced over for a second. "You all right?"

"Yeah, I—" No. "Um, tonight, uh—while I was closing up, um—" She should just start. Tell her the whole twisted story. "Look, uh—"

she let out her breath. "We have to do it again."

Now Jill looked away from the television. *"What?"*

"Yeah," Dorothy said.

Jill glanced at the television, then took her glasses off. "We can't. She was going to be the last one."

"Yeah, I know, but—" Dorothy sighed. *"This* will be the last one, okay?"

Jill sighed too. "You sure?"

Dorothy nodded.

"Okay," Jill said, and closed her French book. "When?"

Preferably, an hour ago. "After school tomorrow?" Dorothy said.

Jill thought about that, then nodded. "Okay. Who is it, anyway?"

"Matt Wilson," Dorothy said.

Jill grinned. "Whoa. *That* must be a long story."

Very long. Dorothy nodded.

"Well—tell me at the commercial," Jill said, then looked at her. "This *is* going to be the last one, right?"

Dorothy nodded.

"Good," Jill said, and put her glasses back on.

Then they both looked at the television.

How We Did It

by Sadie & Bessie Delany

Sadie and Bessie Delany lived together their entire lives. In 1993, the sisters cooperated with a journalist in writing a book called Having Our Say: The Delany Sisters' First 100 Years. *The book was turned into a successful Broadway play.*

People ask us how we've lived so long, how we got where we did. Well, the key is leading a disciplined life. If you're young, that means working or studying hard. When you're our age, it means exercising every day whether you feel like it or not. A lot of people cringe when they hear the word "discipline." They think it means having no fun. Well, that ain't true, and we're living proof! We have a good time.

Some folks today want to do things the easy way. We have a saying, "They want to get there—without going!" And there isn't any such thing. You've got to pay your dues. You've got to work for it.

Sometimes folks ask us how we put up with racism and sexism to get our advanced college degrees. How could we stand it? Well, what choice did we have? What choice does anyone have? Life's not easy for anyone, despite how it may look. Sometimes you just have to put up with a lot to get the little bit you need.

Now, it's true that you hear of basketball stars and entertainers making it big with no education. But that's only a tiny, tiny number of people. And it's sad, because a lot of them are too ignorant to know how to live well with their money.

If you are not educated—if you can't write clearly, speak articulately, think logically—you have lost control of your own life.

Aesop's Last Fable

by William March

Some people just don't know when to shut up.

Aesop, the messenger of King Croesus, finished his business with the Delphians, and went back to the tavern where he had taken lodgings. Later, he came into the taproom where a group of Delphians were drinking. When they realized who he was, they crowded about him. "Tell us," they began, "is Croesus as rich as people say?"

Aesop, since the habit of speaking in fables was so strongly fixed in him, said, "I can best answer your question with a parable, and it is this: The animals gathered together to crown their richest member king. Each animal in turn stated what he possessed, and it was soon apparent that the lion had the largest hunting preserves, the bee the most honey, the squirrel the largest supply of acorns, and so on; but when the voting began, the difficulty of arriving at a decision was plain to all, for to the bee, the nuts that represented the wealth of the squirrel were of no consequence; to the lion, the hay that the zebra and the buffalo owned was worthless; and the panther and the tiger set no value at all on the river that the crane and crocodile prized so highly."

Then Aesop called for his drink, looking into the faces of the Delphians with good-natured amusement. He said, "The moral of the fable is this: Wealth is an intangible thing, and its meaning is not the same to all men alike." The stolid Delphians looked at one another, and when the silence was becoming noticeable, one of them tried again: "How was the weather in Lydia when you left home?"

"I can best answer that question with another fable," said Aesop, "and it is this: During a rain storm, when the ditches were flooded and the ponds had overflowed their banks, a cat and a duck met on the road, and, wanting to make conversation, they spoke at the same instant. 'What a beautiful day this is,' said the delighted duck. 'What terrible weather we're having,' said the disgusted cat."

Again the Delphians looked at one another, and again there was silence. "The moral of that tale," said Aesop, "is this: What pleases a duck, distresses a cat." He poured wine into his glass and leaned against the wall, well satisfied with the start he had made in instructing the barbarous Delphians. The Delphians moved uneasily in their seats, and after a long time, one of them said, "How long are you going to be here?"

"That," said Aesop, "can best be answered in the Fable of the Tortoise, the Pelican, and the Wolf. You see, the pelican went to visit his friend the tortoise, and promised to remain as long as the latter was building his new house. Then one day as they were working together, with the tortoise burrowing and the pelican carrying away the dirt in his pouch, the wolf came on them unexpectedly, and—"

But Aesop got no farther, for the Delphians had surrounded him and were, an instant later, carrying him toward the edge of the cliff on which the tavern was built. When they reached it, they swung him outward and turned him loose, and Aesop was hurled to the rocks below, where he died. "The moral of what we have done," they explained later, "is so obvious that it needs no elaboration!"

Chinese Hot Pot

by Wing Tek Lum

My dream of America
is like *dá bìn lòuh*
with people of all persuasions and tastes
sitting down around a common pot
chopsticks and basket scoops here and there
some cooking squid and others beef
some tofu or watercress
all in one broth
like a stew that really isn't
as each one chooses what he wishes to eat
only that the pot and fire are shared
along with the good company
and the sweet soup
spooned out at the end of the meal.

(Acknowledgements continued from page 2)

"Henry the Kid" by Geoffrey C. Ward. Reprinted by permission of *American Heritage Magazine,* a division of Forbes, Inc. © Forbes, Inc., 1990.

"Wrestling to Lose" by Geof Hewitt, reprinted from *Just Words* by permission of the author. Copyright © 1992 by Geof Hewitt.

"The Scholarship Jacket" by Marta Salinas, from *Nosotras: Latina Literature Today,* ed. by Maria del Carmen Boza, Beverly Silva, and Carmen Valle. Copyright © 1986 by Bilingual Press/Editorial Bilingue. Reprinted with permission of Bilingual Press, Arizona State University, Tempe, AZ.

"A Letter to Eileen" by Harry Noden, reprinted by permission of the author. All rights reserved.

"Flash Cards" from *Grace Notes* by Rita Dove. Copyright © 1989 by Rita Dove. Reprinted by permission of the author and W.W. Norton & Company, Inc.

"The Climb of a Lifetime" from *Above and Beyond* from the Library of Curious and Unusual Facts by the Editors of Time-Life Books. Copyright © 1992 Time-Life, Inc.

"The Children's Wing" by Joyce Johnson, originally appeared in *Harper's.* Copyright © 1986 by Joyce Johnson. Reprinted by permission of the author.

"Kids Taking Care of Kids" by Linda L. Creighton. Copyright, December 20, 1993, *U.S. News & World Report.* Reprinted by permission.

"Where Have You Gone," "The Rebel," "Spectrum," from *I Am a Black Woman,* published by William Morrow & Co., 1970. Reprinted with permission of the author.

"My Mother and Mitch" by Clarence Major, originally appeared in *Fun & Games,* Holy Cow! Press. Copyright © 1990 by Clarence Major. Reprinted by permission of Holy Cow! Press, Duluth, MN.

"August Afternoon" by Nancy Remaly, originally appeared in *English Journal,* May 1976. Copyright © 1976 by the National Council of Teachers of English. Reprinted with permission.

"Caged Bird" from *Shaker, Why Don't You Sing?* by Maya Angelou. Copyright © 1983 by Maya Angelou. Reprinted by permission of Random House, Inc.

"The Man Who Almost Married a Witch," from *The Last Tales of Uncle Remus* by Julius Lester. Copyright © 1994 by Julius Lester. Used by permission of Dial Books for Young Readers, a division of Penguin Books USA, Inc.

"The Lottery" by Shirley Jackson. Copyright © 1948, 1949 by Shirley Jackson. Copyright renewed © 1976, 1977 by Laurence Hyman, Barry Hyman, Mrs. Sarah Webster, and Mrs. Joanne Schnurer. Reprinted by permission of Farrar, Straus & Giroux.